Other Titles by Ralph Moody
Available in Bison Book Editions

LITTLE BRITCHES
MAN OF THE FAMILY
THE FIELDS OF HOME
THE HOME RANCH
MARY EMMA & COMPANY
SHAKING THE NICKEL BUSH
HORSE OF A DIFFERENT COLOR

The Dry Divide

By RALPH MOODY

Illustrated by Tran Mawicke

University of Nebraska Press
Lincoln and London

First Bison Book printing: 1994
Most recent printing indicated by the last digit below:
10   9   8   7   6   5

Library of Congress Cataloging-in-Publication Data
Moody, Ralph, 1898–
The dry divide / by Ralph Moody; illustrated by Tran Mawicke.
p.   cm.
"Bison book editions."
ISBN 0-8032-8216-8 (pbk.)
I. Title.
PS3563.05535D78   1994
813'.54—dc20
94-14522   CIP

Reprinted by arrangement with Edna Moody Morales and Jean S. Moody.

The University of Nebraska Press is grateful to the Lincoln City Libraries
for assistance in the reprinting of this book.

∞

TO
DOC

Contents

THE DRY DIVIDE

1

Ragtag Crew

My luck had always run in ups and downs, sort of like riding a seesaw. But on the Fourth of July, 1919, I hit bottom as if the rider on the other end of the board had suddenly jumped off.

At midnight on the third I was in St. Joseph, Missouri, down to my last dime, and had only one hope left. If I could get to the Fourth of July roundup in Littleton, Colorado I'd find plenty of old friends there, and could easily get a job as a cowhand. Back in 1910, at the time my father died, I'd been a kid trick-rider in that roundup. But there was only one way I could get to Littleton, and that was by hopping the night mail train for Denver. I hopped it just as it pulled out of the depot, flipping onto the blind end of the baggage car right behind the engine, but my luck seemed to have run out, clear down to the last drop. The fireman spied me when I came aboard, and he was at least twice my size. It seemed prudent to accept his suggestion that I shovel coal into the engine for the rest of the night. I did, and was kicked off at McCook, Nebraska the next morning.

Weighing barely a hundred pounds, and having incipient

11

diabetes, I hadn't been in the very best of shape for shoveling coal all night, and my high-heeled boots hadn't been much help to me. My back felt as though it were broken, I was so hungry I was trembling, and my hands and feet were raw with blisters. Besides, any chance of getting to the roundup was gone, and if I didn't find some kind of job in a hurry I was going to be in a bad way.

Although it was early forenoon, the sun was scorching hot, and behind the depot there was a little green lawn, with a stunted cottonwood tree at the center. It looked as good to me as an oasis must look to a man lost in a desert. I hobbled over to it, lay down in the shade of the tree, and must have gone to sleep within two seconds. When I woke up the sun was almost straight overhead, the shade had moved away from me, and my back, legs, and arms were nearly as stiff as though they'd been set in plaster casts. I crawled over to the tree, leaned my aching back against the trunk, and tried to think what I should do next, but I could think only of how hungry I was.

At first I was determined that I wouldn't spend my dime, for a man is never broke while he has a dime left in his pocket, but it's hard to stay determined when you're as hungry as I was. After a few minutes I fished out my dime, tossed it high, and told myself that if it came down heads-up I'd go and get coffee and doughnuts; if it came down tails-up I'd remain a capitalist. It came down tails-up, but I was still awfully hungry, so I told myself I'd make it two out of three, and tossed it up again. And again it came down tails-up. There was no sense in tempting fate any further, so I compromised. I decided to skip the coffee, but have two doughnuts and water. That would still leave me a nickel to hold me over until I could find some sort of job.

When I went into the little hole-in-the-wall restaurant across from the depot, two railroad men were sitting at the counter, having coffee and doughnuts, and talking to the fat counter man about the wheat ripening early that year. I went a few stools farther on, sat down, and ordered doughnuts and a glass of water. Instead of bringing them to me, the counter man put two doughnuts on a plate, and skidded it toward me. Then he filled a glass with water, skidded it my way, and asked in a squeaky voice, "Pitcher?"

I thought he was asking if I wanted a pitcher of water, so just shook my head, then paid no further attention until I'd finished my doughnuts, and heard one of the railroaders say, "I hear the wheat's a'ready ripe on some of them high Kansas divides. Any of them big growers been in for harvest hands yet?"

"A few," the counter man told him, "but they don't come way over here less'n they're looking for topnotch pitchers and stackers, or less'n their reputation's so bad they can't hire no help close to home. There's one or two of 'em . . ."

That's as far as he got. Right at that moment the screen door opened, and for a couple of seconds I thought it must be William Jennings Bryan who was coming in. The man's bushy hair duck-tailed up under the wide brim of his hat in the same way, and he was dressed as I would have expected Bryan to be: a frock coat, striped trousers, a stand-up collar, and a flowing bow tie. He had no more than pulled the door open before he spoke, and his voice filled the little room so full that the walls seemed to vibrate.

"Gentlemen! Gentlemen!" he orated. "May I present myself: Doctor J. Holloway Merriweather, benefactor of mankind and dispenser of the elixir of longevity. Gentlemen, I have a purpose! Show me a man without a purpose, and I will show you a man without . . ."

I hadn't heard a medicine-man spiel since I was a youngster, and was fascinated by it, but the fat counter man wasn't. "If you come in here for a handout, Doc," he squeaked, "you come to the wrong place. Beat it!"

Instead of getting out, Dr. J. Holloway advanced with all the dignity of a Southern gentleman whose honor has been attacked. He rapped his knuckles against the counter, and intoned, "My dear fellow man, I ask no largess. I assure you that any comfort and sustenance accorded me shall be repaid tenfo. . . ."

He was interrupted by a big, rawboned man who stepped into the doorway and shouted, "Any harvest hands been in, Pete?"

"There ain't today, Myron," the counter man called back, "it being the Fourth o' July and all, but I'll keep an eye peeled for you. What you paying?"

"Five for drivers, seven for pitchers, and I'd go as high as eight or nine for a topnotch stacker," the man told him.

I didn't know anything about stacking wheat, but I'd pitched plenty of hay, and wanted a job so bad I didn't dare let the man ask if I'd had any experience. I thought it would be best to put on a bold front, so I called out, "I'll take that stacking job, but not for less than nine dollars a day."

Before the man could say whether or not he'd take me, Dr. J. Holloway Merriweather's voice boomed out, "My good man, albeit below the dignity of my profession, I offer my services as driver of one of your . . . ah . . . conveyances, at the paltry stipend of five dollars per diem."

The farmer looked at Dr. J. Holloway as blankly as if he'd been speaking a foreign language, but one of the railroaders helped him out. "What Doc means is that he's dead broke and stranded. Last night he come aboard the Denver mail train at St. Joe, making out to be a postal inspector, but Bill Hawley smelt a mouse—and his breath—'fore they was ten minutes out of the depot. They kicked him off here this morning. What he wants is a job driving header barge, and he'll take anything you pay him."

"No, no, my good man," J. Holloway interrupted, "not less than five dollars per diem."

No one paid any attention to Doc, but one of the railroaders told the farmer, "The good harvest hands ain't started coming in yet, not this far north, but a few green horns come in on the last freight. They was still hangin' around the yards when we come over for coffee. You might find a couple amongst 'em that wouldn't be too bad."

The farmer didn't answer, but looked back at me, and ordered, "Wait here, stacker!"

He'd barely gone before the railroaders got up and started out. Halfway to the door, one of them turned back and asked, "Wasn't that Hudson, from over on the high divide?"

"That's him," the counter man answered, and there was an inflection in his voice that said a lot more than the words.

Windy as Doc was, and fraud that I knew him to be, I couldn't help feeling a bit sorry for him. Even if he hadn't shoveled coal all night, I knew he must be about as hungry as I'd been, and I didn't think he had a chance of either finding a job or mooching anything to eat. Besides, there was no need of my holding onto my last nickel any longer. Farmer women always set a good table, particularly at harvest time, and even if I fell down on the stacking job and got fired after the first day, I'd get at least enough pay to see me through to Colorado. As soon as the screen door had banged shut, I called to the counter man, "Two more doughnuts, please."

I intended to invite Doc back to have one of them, but there was no need of it. As the plate came skidding down the counter, he followed it like a bloodhound on a fresh scent. He sat down on the next stool to mine, leaned toward me with his eyes fixed on the doughnuts, and whispered confidentially, "I trust you will pardon this intrusion, my dear friend, but I find myself emboldened by the ravages of starvation. Due to adversities quite beyond . . ."

"Never mind the adversities, but have a doughnut," I told him. "I just had two, and they'll last me till I get to the supper table."

Doc wolfed down the doughnuts ravenously, and during the hour till Hudson came back, he told me in flowing oratory the cause of his adversities—leaving out the fact that he'd been on a colossal bender. Since early spring he'd been working southward along the Missouri River with his own medicine show. He claimed to have had a fine pair of horses, a specially built show wagon, a couple of trained poodles, and a dancing girl. But at St. Joseph fortune had turned against him. He was taken with a seizure, and the dancing girl made off with the poodles while he was, "desperately ill, hovering on the brink of death."

Then, in his "delirium" he had made the unfortunate mistake of pasting Elixir of Longevity labels on a gross of bottles filled with his Wonderworker horse liniment. The sale had been tremendous, but some of his customers had been in such a hurry to prolong their lives that they'd sampled their purchases before he could get out of town. They'd run to the police, some of them even claiming their gizzards had been singed, and a heartless minion of the law had stripped him of all his worldly possessions in settlement of their fallacious claims. He was on his way back to Montana, where judges were more tolerant of mistakes, and the populace less tender in the gullet.

I was having so much fun listening to Doc's eloquence that I forgot about Hudson until the counter man squeaked, "How'd you make out, Myron? Scare up enough hands to start harvesting tomorrow?"

"If you'd call 'em hands!" Hudson told him angrily. "Worthless a bunch of bums as ever I seen!" Then he looked back at Doc and me, and shouted, "Come on, you! I ain't got all day to waste!"

If I hadn't been dead broke I'd have told him to go fly his kite, but I didn't. Instead, I said to Doc, "Let's go. We can stick it out for one day, and that will give us enough to get to Denver on."

When Doc and I followed Hudson out to the street I couldn't help agreeing that his crew looked a bit worthless. And I knew what he didn't: that with the possible exception of Doc, I was probably the most worthless one in the bunch. They were gathered around a topless, dilapidated old Maxwell touring car, and looked more like the side-show people from a carnival than a harvest crew.

One of them was a dried-up little man, barely over five feet tall, who couldn't have weighed more than ninety pounds, or been less than sixty years old. Beside him were two hulking great men, more than double his weight, and well over a foot taller. There was no doubting that they were Swedes and brothers, both in their middle forties, and carrying bedrolls half as big as themselves. Standing to one side, their faces as eager as if they were starting off on a holiday, were two boys about my age, and I didn't need to see the D.U. pennants stuck to their suitcases to know were college boys. Both were wearing brand new straw hats, and their trench boots and khaki coveralls couldn't have been out of an army surplus store for more than two days. To complete the motley collection, there was a Mexican boy, not over seventeen or eighteen, and a chunky little Irishman, with a pug nose and a twinkle in his eye.

For the past week the newspapers had been filled with news of the Versailles Treaty and the forming of the League of Nations, and the Irishman must have been reading them. He looked around as Doc and I followed Hudson out of the restaurant, then turned to the college boys and sang out, "Jaikus Jack, lads! 'Tis the League o' Nations we've j'ined. Look what's comin' now!"

Hudson was in no mood for joking. He yanked the crank up to start the engine, jackknifed in behind the steering wheel, and ordered, "You big ones get in! The rest of you'll ride the running boards, and you'll walk the hills."

Doc needed no ordering. He was already clambering into the front seat, with the air of a condescending senator who knows himself entitled to the place of honor. The springs of the old Maxwell groaned as the two big Swedes settled on the back seat. By the time the bedrolls, suitcases, and odd dunnage had been piled around their knees, the back end was filled level with the door tops, but Hudson looked around at the little man and snapped, "Get in with the Swedes!"

Little as the old fellow was, he'd have been smothered if he'd tried to wedge himself in between those two behemoths, so he perched on top of the dunnage, looking like a monkey in a circus parade. Hudson raced the engine, nearly stripped the gears out of the old jalopy, and we creaked away—the two college boys clinging gleefully to one side; the Mexican boy, the Irishman, and I, apprehensively to the other.

As soon as we'd pulled out of town, Doc tried to start a conversation with Hudson, but he never got even a grunt in reply. The Irishman chattered like a magpie; asking our names, where we were from, and anything else he could think of— all in a brogue so thick I could hardly understand him. Only Edgar and Everett, the college boys, seemed willing to put out any information. For the past seven months my partner had called me Buddy, and I'd become used to the name, so I simply said I was Bud. And to my surprise, Dr. J. Holloway Merriweather said, "Just call me Doc."

The two big Swedes looked straight ahead, with no expression on their faces, and the only sign they gave of having heard the Irishman's questions was when one said, "Gus," and the other, "Lars."

The little man gave his name as Bill Weaver, and the Mexican boy looked confused and a bit frightened. I guessed that he might not know a word of English, so asked, "*Como se llama?*"

His face brightened as if he'd just found an old friend from home. He flashed a smile up at me and said, "Paco," then added, almost questioningly, "amigo mio."

I'd picked up a little Spanish when I was a kid working on the ranches, and when I heard that bit of question in Paco's voice, "*Para siempre,*" (always) came out as easily as if I'd been speaking the language every day. From then on Paco was my boy, and though he left me way behind if he got excited and talked too fast, we had no trouble in understanding each other.

Every time the Irishman saw something that caught his attention he'd shout, "Jaikus Jack!" so that's what we called him—either that or Jaikus. Hudson stood his babbling for maybe three or four minutes, then half turned his head and bellowed, "Shut up!" I couldn't blame him much, but I thought I knew why he'd had to come to McCook for a harvest crew, and had taken anything he could get.

For the first mile our road lay southward across the Republican River valley, between fields of shoulder-high corn. Then it wound like a tortured snake up a steep, rough gulch to the top of a high divide. As soon as Hudson shifted into second gear, those of us on the running boards dropped off. Jaikus, Paco, and I started plodding up the roadway behind the roaring, rattling jalopy, but the college boys capered away like a pair of colts let out to pasture, evidently set on beating the Maxwell to the opposite side of the switchback. They'd taken no more than half a dozen bounds before Hudson yelled, "Get back, you fools! There's rattlers in them gulches!"

The boys scrambled wildly back to the roadway, then it dawned on Everett that they'd been insulted, and he shouted, "Stop! We're quitting and want our suitcases. Stop! Stop, I tell . . ."

Hudson paid no attention, but Edgar grabbed Everett's arm, and shushed him. If he'd yelled it out, he couldn't have told us any more clearly that they were dead broke, and had spent their last dimes for their outfits.

It was nearly a mile to the top of that gulch, and by the time I got there the blisters on my heels were howling, but Edgar and Everett were in even worse shape. From the way they hobbled and fell behind, it was easy to see that their new trench boots were giving them fits. And Hudson added to their torture by swearing at them and yelling for them to hurry.

From the top of the gulch, the land stretched away as far as I could see in a gently rolling series of low hills, cut here and there by shallow draws, deep gulches, and ravines, and was almost equally divided between corn, wheat, and pasture. But up there on the divide the corn was only waist high, and the leaves were curled tight against the heat. The road was little more than a pair of wheel tracks, rounded up a bit at the center, and followed straight southward along the section line, regardless of what lay in its path. If Hudson hadn't driven like a lunatic, so those of us on the running boards had to hang on for our lives, and if we hadn't had to climb half a dozen hills afoot, I might have enjoyed that drive.

Where the land was broken by gulches and ravines, whole sections were fenced off for pasture. Other sections stretched away in billowing, golden seas; one wave following another across them as the ripening wheat swayed and nodded in the hot wind that swept above it. To me there was something fascinating about it, as it caught and reflected the sunlight in countless shades of yellow, and brown, and gold. I had seen wheat fields before, ripe ones, but they had always been beardless wheat, brown and shimmerless. This wheat was bearded like barley, and it was from the long, spinelike quills that the sunlight was reflected.

We had gone about twenty miles, nearly straight southward, when we crossed the state line into Kansas. For the next mile the land sloped away to a green valley, about half a mile wide, with cottonwoods and alders marking the course of a creek that wound and twisted through it. At the far side of the valley a little town of not more than twenty houses nestled at the foot of lofty, rolling hills. To the east of it stood high limestone bluffs, where the creek had cut deep into a hillside, and atop the highest point of the bluff a gnarled old cedar stood sentinel. Skirting the foot of the bluff and drawing a line between the town and the level floor of the valley, there was a single-track railway.

On a railroad siding to the east stood two tall red grain elevators, beyond them a little lumber yard, and farther on, shipping pens for livestock. To the west there was a red depot, with a sign CEDAR BLUFFS on the front. The main street was a single block long, the buildings all peak-roofed and clapboard sided, but a few had square false fronts. At the far end there was a bank, little more than twenty feet square, the windows painted in big letters, FIRST STATE BANK. The

business block was lifeless as we rolled through the town, but eight or ten carriages and buckboards were lined up at the hitching rail in front of the schoolhouse, and as we passed the voices of singing children came from the open windows.

At the schoolhouse our road turned sharply and zigzagged up a steep hill that rose high above the bluffs. By the time I'd climbed to the top my blisters were singing louder than the youngsters in the schoolhouse. But even at that, the view from the hilltop was worth the climb. I'd never seen a more beautiful, or greener, valley than the one stretched out beneath me.

The divide we had climbed was higher and drier than the first one we'd crossed. Here and there hills were piled high, with deep valleys and gullies between them. In other places the hillsides were ripped and torn by deep gulches, but the farther we went toward the top of the divide the less the land was broken. There the hills flattened out until a few sections lay almost as flat as a floor, cut only by a shallow gulch or two. And wherever the land was not too steep or badly cut, it gleamed golden with waving fields of ripening wheat.

Where the top of the divide flattened out, seven or eight miles southeast of the town, Hudson turned off the road, and followed a set of wheel ruts toward a windmill that stood high above the waving sea of grain. Otherwise I wouldn't have noticed the tiny cottage that stood at the base of the mill, or the low, weather blackened barn and corral. Two mongrel dogs raced out to challenge us, barking wildly as we pulled into a barren, sun-baked yard, littered with worn-out farm machinery and a miscellaneous assortment of junk. At one side there was a tumble-down shed-roofed barn, and a corral with four droop-headed horses in it. On the other side was the windmill, a water tank, and a two-room house—once white—with a blackened lean-to kitchen at the back.

Lined up in front of the house, and watching us as if they realized what a motley crew we were, stood four barefooted and dirty children—a boy about two years old, and three girls ranging up to one about eight. As Hudson swung the old

Maxwell in a circle and brought it to a stop, the youngsters broke and ran to the back of the house like frightened rabbits. The jalopy had barely jolted to a stop when Hudson jumped out, grabbed up a club, fired it at the dogs, and followed it with the loudest, longest, and most vehement swearing I'd heard in years. He missed the dogs, but they seemed to understand the language, and raced away to hide under the house. Then he turned back to us just long enough to say, "Straw stack's behind the barn," and strode off to the house.

Gus and Lars knew what he meant as well as I did. As soon as the dunnage had been unloaded they picked up their bedrolls and trudged away toward the barn. Old Bill and Jaikus gathered up their bundles and followed, but Edgar and Everett stood, suitcases in hand, looking as puzzled as if they'd suddenly found themselves on the moon. "The hotel's behind the barn," I told them, "but there's no chambermaid; you'll have to make your own beds." I didn't say it sarcastically, but they seemed to take it that way, shot me a pair of haughty looks, and limped away behind the others.

I didn't notice Paco until the boys had gone, and the first thing that caught my eye was the beautiful Indian blanket that he carried, rolled tightly at full width, tied with rawhide thongs, and slung over his shoulder in the shape of a horseshoe. He was standing by the empty jalopy, glanced into it, then looked up at Doc and me questioningly and spread his hands, palms up. There was no need of his asking what had become of our bedrolls and luggage, and there was no reason for my explaining. I just shrugged my shoulders a fraction of an inch and told him to go with the others.

2

Blacksnake

WITH the rest of the crew gone to make their beds, Doc and I were left standing alone in the center of the desolate yard. He bowed to me as though he were addressing an audience, swept an arm around in an elegant gesture, and declaimed in a resonant voice, "Behold the Promised Land!" Then, dropping his voice enough that it wouldn't reach the house, he went on, "My dear companion of adversity, I fear that Fortune still turns her beaming face against us, and has cast us like pearls before swine."

"Well, if we're pearls, we're certainly imitations," I told him, "and right now I'm hungry enough that I'd be glad to be cast before swine—plenty of it—fried, and with potatoes and gravy. What I can't figure is how we're going to harvest any wheat with the junk lying around this yard and those four old nags in the corral. How did a man like this one get a ranch in the first place, or a crop planted on it after he had it?"

"Share cropper!" Doc told me. "Share cropper of low degree, a mere vassal of the landlord and the banker, driven to the summit of this bleak and barren divide by the exigencies of poverty."

It seemed to me that Doc was letting himself be carried away by the eloquence of his oratory, for we were surrounded by hundreds of acres of knee-high golden wheat, so I said, "I don't see anything bleak about this divide. It looks to me like the finest wheat country that lies outdoors."

I think Doc resented my disagreeing with him, but I think he remembered eating my doughnuts, too. He linked an arm in mine, led me toward the corral, and told me in a patronizing voice, "Ah, my dear young friend, you speak from unenlightenment. But two years in seven the eye of God rests upon these high divides, and in grief at their desolation He sheds tears of compassion upon them to bring forth harvest. In years of drought only the soaring buzzards look down upon them, and the lowly raven needs must carry rations to span their wide expanse. But come, let us survey the establishment. It appears that our employer has been readying his barges and header for the bountiful harvest."

I had no idea what Doc meant by barges and header. I'd seen wheat harvested, but always with a binder that cut the grain and tied it into sheaves. The machine Doc led me to looked as if it had been put together backwards, for I could see that it would be pushed ahead of the horses, rather than being pulled behind them. The frame was in the shape of a T, with the crossbar, or axle, supported by great, wide-flanged wheels. The end of the tail was supported by a steering post, with a small swivel wheel at the bottom and a rudder at the top. And tripletrees attached below the rudder showed that six horses would be used, three on each side of the tail.

Mounted in front of the axle, and hung from it by cantilever arms, so it could be raised or lowered by a boom pole, was the harvesting machinery. There was a jagged-toothed cutter bar, about fifteen feet wide, with a revolving reel above it for pushing the cut grain back onto a canvas conveyor belt. At one end of that conveyor there was another, rising at an angle and held in place by a crane with ropes and pulleys. And all the moving parts were connected to the great driving wheel by a series of sprockets, gears, and chains.

It was easy enough to see that the wheat wouldn't be bound into bundles, but carried along the conveyors just as it fell, and dumped loose into the wagons that I supposed were called barges. I didn't want even Doc to know how ignorant I was about harvesting, so I didn't pay much attention to his orating about the age and bad condition of the old header. Instead I tried to figure out how it worked, and what chains and sprockets turned which parts. I was still trying to figure it out when I heard the engine of the old Maxwell start with a roar. There was a screeching of gears, and Hudson drove out of the yard as if he were headed for a fire.

I watched him race down the wheel ruts to the corner, turn it in a cloud of flying dust, and streak away to the west. Then I turned to Doc and said, "I wonder where he's going in such a hurry."

He straightened up, settled the frock coat more snugly on his shoulders, and announced in his most vibrant tone, "My dear companion, lacking clairvoyant powers I find myself unable to throw light upon this sudden and strange departure, but on pretext of seeking elucidation I shall call upon the fair mistress of yon manor house. And, preadventure she prove affable, shall procure raiment more fitting to the arduous occupation which confronts me on the morrow."

Whatever Doc lacked in honest piety he could make up for in benign expression, and when he walked slowly away toward the dingy little house he looked for all the world like a visiting preacher. He was gone for maybe fifteen minutes, while I looked over what I knew must be the barges for hauling wheat from the header to the stacks. They were rickety, weather blackened platforms, fenced around the edges by slats, and three or four feet higher on one side than the other. Many of the slats were broken or missing, but fresh hammer marks showed where a few rusty nails had been driven into the half rotten floor boards.

The barges lay flat on the ground, and behind them three

blackened running gears lay equally flat—wheelless, and with
the hub spindles crusted by dried-out grease from the previous
summer. In the corral two old bay mares and two runty mustangs stood, heads hanging down, and tails switching at the
flies, but there was no haystack or other sign of feed for them.
I'd forgotten about Doc, and was looking at the horses when
I heard a voice that sounded like his, but without the deep-
throated vibrance, call, "Hey, Bud! Come here a minute!"

Doc was standing in the barn doorway when I looked around,
wearing a tattered blue shirt and patched old overalls. As soon
as I looked his way he motioned to me and went back inside,
so I hurried over there, puzzled enough by his change of voice,
but more by his calling me "Bud," instead of, "My dear companion."

The barn was only a dark shed, with half a dozen double
stalls along one side, a row of delapidated harness hanging on
the opposite wall, and the runway between littered deep with
dried manure. Doc was in the farthest stall, kneeling and
wrapping his neatly folded frock coat, vest, and striped trousers
into a newspaper covered package. As soon as I'd found him
I called, "What's the matter, Doc?" But he didn't answer until
he'd stowed the package carefully on a brace board below the
rafters.

Then he turned to me and said in a quiet voice, "Buddy boy,
this outfit's in a bad way. Either this jasper has been on a
long drunk, or he's crazier'n a hooty owl, else he'd have his
horses in from pasture and his barges together before he hired
a harvest crew. I'm not legging for him, but I sure feel sorry
for that poor woman in there and those little kids. They're as
scared of him as the devil is of holy water, and the woman's
worried sick that he won't get this crop harvested. I found her
in there trying to cut up a hog half the size of a horse, with
a squalling baby under her feet, and one under her apron
that looks to be due almost any time. Hudson has gone for
her kid sister, Judy, and I'm going in to cut up that hog for her.
Why don't you get the boys together and set up those barges?"

If Doc had spread wings and flown I couldn't have been more bewildered. It didn't seem possible that he could have packed his oratory away with his medicine-man clothes, but I liked him much better without it—and I liked him even more for what he'd said. It struck me so quick and hard that I couldn't think straight for a few seconds. I just stood there like a dummy, then said, "Sure. Sure, Doc. But I didn't see any wheels for the wagons."

"Probably in the water tank, getting soaked up so they won't fall apart the first day," Doc told me as he started for the doorway. Then he called back, "There's a bucket of axle grease there in the corner, and a hub wrench hanging above it."

When I went behind the barn to call the crew I could see why Gus and Lars had been carrying such big bedrolls. They'd set themselves up a little tent, covered the floor with about a foot of straw, spread blankets over it, and were having a siesta. Beyond the tent there was a blackened heap of straw, one side of it yellow where clean mattress material had been dug out. Old Bill and Jaikus had laid out narrow beds of straw, covered them with their blankets, and were sitting on them. Beside them was another narrow oblong of straw, and Paco was covering a much wider one with his colorful blanket. Edgar and Everett hadn't bothered to lay out beds for themselves, but had their boots off and were taking a nap in the shade of the barn. "How about giving me a hand at putting the barges together?" I called.

Gus and Lars heaved themselves onto their rumps and reached for their boots, with no more expression on their faces than a couple of sleepy steers. Paco came to me as soon as I spoke, and Jaikus and Bill got to their feet, but Everett and Edgar only propped themselves sulkily on their elbows. Then Everett asked, "Do we get paid for it?"

"No," I told him. "Not a dime, but unless those barges are ready for harvesting, we won't get paid for tomorrow either."

Although I had no right to do any bossing, the other fellows seemed willing enough to have me tell them what to do. We found the wheels in the water tank, just as Doc thought they would be, but they were little more than junk, and no attempt had been made to repair them before they'd been put to soak. While Old Bill, Jaikus, and Paco hunted for baling wire, old nails, and anything we could use for tools, Gus, Lars and I fished the wheels out of the tank. Then we three went to work on them, binding split spokes and hubs with wire, wedging the fellies tight, and pounding them as straight as we could inside the tires. By the time we had the wheels fixed up enough to mount on the running gears, the other fellows had the barges patched up enough to be usable.

We were lifting the last barge onto the running gear, and I had my back to the roadway, when I heard the old Maxwell rattle into the yard behind me. By the time we'd landed our load, so I had a chance to look around, a perky little girl of about eighteen was walking toward the house with a suitcase in her hand. She wasn't taller than five-feet-two, but she carried her head high, and she filled out her gingham dress as prettily as any girl I'd seen in a long, long time.

Hudson paid no more attention to us than if we hadn't been there, but took three pitchforks from the back of the jalopy and started away toward the barn. He'd gone about halfway when he looked back and ordered, "Whichever one of you can ride, help me get the horses in!"

I hadn't been on a horse since riding in falls for the movies the previous November, and I hadn't ridden bareback since I was a boy, but it was certain that whoever went to help Hudson would be riding that way, for there was only one beat-up saddle in the barn, and he was evidently going for it. I'd noticed a split-ear bridle hanging on a post at the corral gate, so when none of the other fellows made a move I went over, took it down, and went in.

The old bay mares paid no attention to me, but the two mustangs whirled and circled toward the back of the corral. The smaller of the two, weighing no more than seven hundred pounds, ducked her tail and kept her face turned toward me.

I knew instantly that she'd been whip broken, so had learned to keep her face toward any man on foot. I swung one bridle rein back as if it had been a whip, but before there was time for it to snap forward the little mare wheeled and stood stock-still facing me. Her ears pinned tight against her neck as I walked toward her, but she didn't snap when I raised the bridle to her head, and she opened her mouth for the bit when I slipped a thumb between her lips. As she did, I noticed that her lower teeth were nearly an inch long, and extended almost horizontally, a sure sign that she was at least thirty years old.

As soon as I'd slipped her ears through the bridle loops I tossed the off rein over her neck, gathered it with the near one, and swung a leg back to vault onto her. I'd barely swung the leg when Hudson yelled, "Stay off that mare!"

It was too late. My leg was already kicking forward, and the momentum sent me flying up to her back. I wasn't there a second.

The instant I landed she reared straight up, and I was lucky that I was bareback instead of in a saddle. I didn't wait to find out if she'd go clear over. In my trick-riding days I'd learned that the only way of curing a horse of going over backwards was to make sure it fell hard and flat on its back, so I jumped clear and yanked the little bronco's head straight back as I went. Quick as she was, she had no chance to twist as she fell, and crashed down hard on her back.

Few horses are in any hurry to get up after a fall like that, but the little mustang rolled over and came to her feet like a cat. With Hudson yelling at me again, I flipped aboard as soon as she had her legs under her, only to go through the same routine a second time.

The bronc was barely on her feet again before Hudson was through the gate and coming toward me, shouting, "I told you to stay off that mare! There can't nobody but me ride her."

There was no doubting that the little bronco had tried to get me that second time. She'd gone up and over all in one motion, bound to take me down under her. If it hadn't been for the recent practice I'd had at fall riding, she'd have done it, too. I barely got clear, and landed as flat as she did. It made me angry enough that I wouldn't have paid any attention to Hudson if he'd been holding a gun on me. Before he was halfway across the corral I flipped onto the mare's back again— and no one could have guessed that she wasn't glad to have me there. Her ears came up, and she stepped away smoothly when I pressed my knees against her. As I reined her past Hudson and toward the gate, I told him, "I'll ride this one." I knew it might start trouble, but I didn't like his yelling at me, and I thought I might as well let him know it. He didn't say a word to me, but he cussed the tar out of the other mustang before he'd caught and saddled her.

Although the little bronco behaved herself beautifully as I rode her out of the corral I didn't trust her. Most horses that try to get a man once will try to get him again, but if the smart ones fail in their first try or two they'll usually wait for a chance to catch their rider napping. And it's when they catch him napping that he really gets hurt. I was watching the bronc so closely that I didn't look up until I was outside the gate, then I might have thought I was riding at a roundup. Hudson's yelling had evidently frightened his wife and her sister. They, Doc, and the four youngsters were standing at the corner of the house, shading their eyes against the late afternoon sun and looking toward the corral. Paco's teeth had flashed white when he swung the gate open for me, and the other fellows stood watching as if they expected another performance as much as I did. There wasn't any.

Hudson came spurring out of the corral at a dead run, a heavy blacksnake whip coiled in one hand. He brushed so close to me that his leg bumped mine, then raced on across the yard. I knew he was trying to set the little bronco off again, but instead she sidestepped and dashed away behind him. It was no more than fifty yards from the corral to the gate of a milking pen at the base of the windmill. At the speed Hudson was riding, I expected him to go right on past the gate, but he didn't. He was within a single length of it when he suddenly yanked his pony's head up viciously and stepped from the saddle. The little mare and I were so close behind that I didn't have time to think, but a man can't think as fast as a topnotch mustang. I barely felt her rump fall away before she'd set her feet and slid to a dead stop. The only thing that saved me from going over her head was that I'd ridden bareback a couple of years before I ever had a saddle, and my knees clutched hold from a memory my head had long forgotten.

The gate was only three strands of barbed wire, twisted around an end pole that was held in place by a couple of loops. Hudson sprung it loose and threw it back onto the ground as though he were taking out his anger at me on it, then stepped into the saddle and raked his horse with the spurs. With dried cow chips flying back in my face, we raced through the milking pen and into a narrow lane that led over a low rise of ground behind the house, my little mare keeping exactly one length behind his.

It was no more than a quarter-mile to the top of the rise, and when we reached it we came out into a half section of pasture, hacked by deep draws and gulches. About half a mile away, where the land pitched downward to the main gulch, a dozen or so horses and three or four colts raised their heads from grazing, then plumed their tails and streaked for the gulch as if they'd been a wild herd.

Until the horses raced out of sight Hudson had shown no sign of knowing I was along. Then, without looking back, he wheeled his pony to the right, waved me in the opposite direction, and yelled, "Head 'em off, and don't leave 'em get by you!"

If a man knows a pasture he has a pretty good idea where horses will run in it, the best place to head them off, and how to get there. But in a pasture he's never seen before, and on land that is badly cut with gulches, he hasn't much chance. I could think of only one sensible thing to do, and it turned out to be the right one. I leaned a bit forward and patted the

smart little mustang's neck a few slaps, just to let her know I
had confidence in her, then turned her loose to take me where-
ever she thought best.

When I was a little kid I used to wish I could talk to horses,
and they to me, but I think it's better just as it is, for among
people it's talking more than anything else that breaks friend-
ships and causes misunderstandings. The little mustang left
me no doubt that she understood. Her ears pinched back, her
muzzle stretched out like the neck of a goose in flight, and she
turned on a burst of speed that I'd have thought impossible
for a horse of her age.

The horse herd had been to the southeast of us, and had
been running northeast when it disappeared, but the little
mare raced straight to the north. In less than half a minute
I could see why she had done it. A narrow ravine extended
far out from the main gulch, its walls dropping straight down,
twenty feet or more. I clamped my legs tight and leaned a
bit, expecting the mare to swerve and circle the end of it,
but she didn't. She drove straight on, met the ravine at the
one spot where it narrowed to a little more than fifteen feet,
sailed across, and landed with hardly a break in the rhythm
of her stride. She'd barely landed before she banked sharply,
and plunged, sliding and bounding, down a second but wider
ravine.

The ravine led into a deep gulch, shaped like a huge bottle,
with walls rising thirty feet on both sides. The neck we had
come into was less than twenty feet wide, but to the south the
gulch widened into a grassy valley, a hundred feet or more
across. Where it narrowed into the neck, a side ravine led off
in the direction of the lane.

As we came into the big gulch I saw the horse herd trotting
toward me in the wide grassy valley, about as far to the south
of the bottleneck as we were to the north, and Hudson was
loping his pony a hundred yards or so behind. We must have
caught sight of each other at the same moment, for I'd barely
seen him before he put his pony into a dead run. Shouting

and lashing the blacksnake till the tip leathers popped like
pistol shots, he closed in behind the heard. As if frightened
by a demon, the horses flung their tails high and came racing
toward me.

I didn't need to be very smart to figure out what Hudson
was up to. If he could catch me in that narrow neck and
stampede the little bronco into throwing me, I'd be ground
into hamburger under the hoofs of the racing herd. I had only
two choices: I could turn tail and get out of there, or I could
race the herd to the neck of the bottle. I dropped Indian-fashion
above the little mare's neck, dug my heels in, and she shot away
like a startled cottontail.

The race was about as close as one can be. For the last hundred yards I could see that we would meet right where the
shoulders of the gulch joined the neck. Coming head-on, and
traveling at the speed we were, it seemed impossible that we
could do anything but crash together, and that my little bronc
must surely go down, but she charged that racing herd like
an infuriated wildcat, head swinging from side to side and
teeth bared.

For the next minute, or maybe less, the action was too fast
for me to do anything but clutch both hands full of mane and
hang on for dear life. A mass of rearing, dodging mustangs
swirled in the bottom of that gulch like wildly boiling paint
in a pot. To me they were hardly more than a blur, for my
little mare was bouncing and whirling like a cat in a fit, and
my head snapped back and forth as though it were mounted
on a limber spring.

The violent action stopped as suddenly as it had begun.
When my head cleared a stream of horses was pouring into
the ravine that led toward the lane, trying to escape the frenzy
of one little thirty-year-old mare—and a fifteen-foot blacksnake whip in the hand of a raw-boned, angry man. For maybe
three seconds Hudson and I sat, no more than a horse length
apart, looking straight into one another's eyes. He raised the
butt of his whip threateningly, then let it fall, and reined his

pony into the ravine behind the herd.

Most horses will head straight for the corral when pointed in that direction, but Hudson's were all mustangs, the wildest I'd ever seen in captivity, and were determined not to be driven to the corral. I didn't need anyone to tell me why. He'd evidently never fed them there, but had abused them so much that they were afraid of confinement. After we'd followed them up from the gulch it took us at least fifteen minutes to get them out of the pasture—Hudson lashing them with the blacksnake from one side, and my little mare raking with her teeth from the other.

Hudson neither looked my way nor spoke until we'd driven the frightened and excited horses into the corral, then he yelled at me, "Watch that gate while I cut the colts back!"

As I tended the gate and the rest of the crew looked on in awe, Hudson rode to the center of the corral, wheeled his pony, and set his whip lashing as if it were actually an infuriated blacksnake. The terrified horses crowded into the farthest corner, but there was no way of escape, no letup in Hudson's lashing—and no missing either. Each time the tail of the whip lashed out it bit hair from a two-year-old, a yearling, or a foal.

Without looking away, Doc asked, "Is the man crazy?"

"I don't think so," I told him. "We had a little go-round in the pasture, and he's mad enough to kill me if he dared. He's taking it out on the colts."

"Then you're crazy," Doc told me, "or you'd be making tracks away from here. Skunk that he is, he's a wizard with that whip. He could cut you into jerky with it in less than two minutes."

"He won't," I said. "Any man who treats animals the way he does is a coward, and there's no reason to be afraid of him."

In panic the horses broke out of the corner, racing around the corral, and as they ran Hudson turned his pony and kept his whip writhing until he had strung them out in single file, whirling like a runaway merry-go-round. I knew well enough what he'd do next, so set my feet, ready to swing the gate open. As a yearling came racing around the end of the corral, Hudson's whip bit it on the head, knocked it off stride, and sent it hurtling toward me. I barely had time to yank the gate open and let it out. He cut the rest of the colts in the same way, one at each turn of the merry-go-round.

With all his brutality, Hudson was an expert with a whip, and there could be no doubt that he'd been showing off for the crew, just as he thought I'd been doing when the mare went over backwards with me. It seemed to me that a little recognition of his skill might help matters between us, so as I swung the gate open for him I looked up and said, loud enough for the other fellows to hear, "You're a crackerjack with that whip."

He glared at me as he rode on past, and growled, "Don't you never forget it neither!" Then he spurred away to drive the colts back to pasture.

Hudson was barely out of hearing before Doc slapped me on the back, and said, "Good going, Bud! I figured I'd have to get you out of here before nightfall, but it looks like the war's over."

"Armistice anyway," I told him, "and it was my place to ask for it. I started the rumpus by riding the bronc after he'd told me not to. She's some horse, for an old one."

"Could you teach a horse that over-backwards trick?" Doc asked.

"Sure," I said, "but it would only ruin him for anything else."

Doc slapped me again, and said eagerly, "I'll tell you what: soon as harvest is over and we've made a little stake, you and I'll go into the medicine-show business, and brother we'll clean up a fortune. We'll get us a couple of gals that can shake a leg, and a show wagon, and you teach a bronc to. . . ."

That's as far as he got. From the windmill platform, Judy called, "Supp—pper!"

3

Judy's Story

WHEN Judy called us to supper she set a tin wash basin on the platform under the windmill, and went back to the house. The rest of the crew hurried away to wash, leaving Doc and me stragglers. He seemed to be in no hurry, and wanted to talk more about our going into the medicine-show business, but I told him, "Keep your shirt on till after supper, Doc. Right now I'm more interested in fried pork and gravy than medicine."

Doc's belly jiggled as he snickered and told me, "You'll get your medicine right along with your supper. That hog I cut up was an old boar, and by the time he's fried he's going to be strong medicine."

I'd forgotten about Doc's having been at the house till he mentioned the hog, so I asked, "What's Judy like?"

"Nice kid," he told me, "but no good for the medicine-show business. You got to have troopers for that game, gals that can pass a bunch of wise-cracks back as good as they send. This kid's all right, though, for a small town girl. Knows how to take hold and get things moving. That poor sister of hers is kind of on the skim milk side, beat out by having one youngster right after another, and if I don't miss my guess she's been doing field work."

While Doc and I were waiting our turn at the wash basin,
Hudson came back from the pasture, driving half a dozen old
milk cows. He didn't look toward us as he closed the lane gate,
but rode on through the milking pen, turned his sweat streaked
pony into the corral, and stalked to the house without coming
near us.

As the other fellows washed, they stood aside, waiting so
that we'd all go in to supper together. And when we went I
lost my appetite. The half-rancid, nauseating smell of old-boar
pork came out to meet us. The kitchen was no more than ten
by twelve feet, with a hot cook stove at one side, and a cream
separator in the far corner. An uncovered table of rough boards
stood in the center of the room, surrounded by a few rickety
chairs, a bench, and a couple of boxes stood on end. Although
the door and windows were wide open, the temperature was
about 120°, and the flies must have liked the smell of boar
pork better than I did. The room was swarming with them.

Ten places had been set at the table, and in the center there
was a bowl of unpeeled boiled potatoes, another of gray milk-
and-flour gravy, two plates of biscuits, a cracked pitcher that
was leaking skimmed milk, a gallon-sized coffee pot, and a
platter of fried side meat. Neither Mrs. Hudson, Judy, nor the
children were in sight, but Hudson was seated at the far end
of the table, shoveling pork and potato into his mouth as though
he were stoking a boiler. He didn't look up as we came in, so
after bunching inside the doorway a few moments we found
ourselves seats, everyone trying to stay as far as possible from
the stove and the boss. Doc and I were the last in, so had to
take seats beside Hudson.

For maybe six or seven minutes the only sounds were the
click of knives against plates, or someone asking, "Pass the
spuds."

Then, from a room beyond a half-closed door behind me, a
child coughed and began to cry. Hudson stopped shoveling
just long enough to turn his head toward the doorway and

yell, "Shut up!" Then he went on with his eating, and the child stopped crying.

With the first whiff of pork, I'd made up my mind that I wasn't going to eat any of it, but I found myself licked. The rest of the meal wasn't exactly planned for a diabetic diet, and the only way I could avoid that pork was by sticking to straight boiled potatoes. The milk pitcher was empty long before it reached me, the coffee was as bitter as gall, and both the gravy and the biscuits had been made with grease from the pork, so they were just as rank tasting as it was. All I could do was to tell myself it wouldn't poison me, and that it would do me less harm than too many potatoes, so I waded in. That pork was sort of like the sulfur and molasses my mother used to give us every spring when we were kids. The first mouthful nearly gagged me, but after I got used to it I could swallow it without too much trouble.

I'd just reached for my third slab of side meat when Hudson pushed his chair back from the table, took a lantern from a nail above the separator, lit it, and went out. The meal had been gloomy enough that I hadn't noticed twilight was deepening until he lit the lantern, and after he'd gone out the gathering darkness seemed restful to me. It must have been the same with the other fellows. Though none of them spoke, the tension seemed to drain away, and one after another they left their half-eaten meal and went outside.

Being farthest from the door, Doc and I were the last ones out. Paco was waiting at the corner of the house, in the dusk I could see the others straggling away to our camp behind the barn, and a yellow speck of lantern light showed that Hudson was at the header. The wind had gone down with the sun, leaving behind it a void of silence and breathless heat, broken only by an occasional clink of metal at the header. Weary as I was, there seemed no sense in going to lie and sweat on a mattress of prickly straw. Doc must have felt as I did, for without a word he turned toward the windmill, and I went with him, Paco trailing a step or two behind. The mill tower stood on a plank platform about a foot above the ground, just the right height for men to sit restfully, elbows on their knees. And when a man is resting there's no reason to talk.

Gradually the twilight faded to darkness, broken only by the gleam from Hudson's lanterns and a yellow shaft that reached out across the ground from the kitchen doorway. So slowly it was barely noticeable, the eastern sky lightened until the shape of the land stood black against it, turned a faint pink, then deepened to a dusky rose that glowed and expanded as though, far beyond the horizon, there might be an enormous prairie fire. Like a low bank of flame at its center, the dome of the full moon pushed upward, blood red above the black outline of the land.

Steadily the crimson ball rose as if a mighty power were forcing it reluctantly from the molten center of the earth. For a few seconds it seemed balanced atop the motionless sea of wheat that stretched away in front of us. Then majestically it sailed free of its anchorage, spilling its light across the silent, sweltering divide. And as if it had been waiting only for the moonlight, a gentle breeze sprang up to rustle the bearded heads of the wheat with a hushed, whispering sound.

As the moon had risen the only sounds had been the occasional clink of dishes being washed in the kitchen, or the stamp of a horse's hoof in the corral. But with the rising of the breeze the oppressive burden of the heat, and the silence were broken. Far away to the south a coyote voiced his lonesome, wailing evening song. Locusts and crickets tuned their shrill fiddles in the wheat fields, a colt whinnied from the pasture, and from right behind us a cow bellowed; the long, low bawl of a milker distressed by an overfull udder. With the silence violated, Doc turned toward me, and asked, "How your blisters doing, Bud? Going to be in shape for handling a pitchfork tomorrow?"

"That won't bother the blisters that are biting me worst," I told him. "It's ten years since I've ridden a horse bareback."

Doc chuckled, and asked, "Seen any rock salt around?"

"There's a block at the end of the pasture lane," I told him. "Let's go get a chunk of it," he said. "You'll need to harden those hands or you'll set them to bleeding by noontime."

We'd just gotten to our feet when Mrs. Hudson came out of the kitchen doorway, two milk buckets in her hands, and started for the milking pen. Her shoulders sagged wearily, as though the buckets were already full and the child she carried were burdensome. I hadn't milked a cow since before the war, but I'd never minded milking, so I told Doc, "You go ahead and get the salt; I'll give the lady a hand with the milking. She looks beat out."

As we turned away Paco stood for a moment between us, confused by the conversation he couldn't understand, then followed at my heels as though he were a puppy. As I neared Mrs. Hudson, I said, "I'm Bud, one of the harvest hand, and I like to milk. Would you mind if Paco and I did it tonight?"

At the sound of my voice she jumped as if frightened, then stopped and turned toward me, with the moonlight full on her face. For a second or two she stood looking bewildered, her mouth partly open as if she wanted to speak but couldn't think of the words. She wet her lips nervously, and half stammered, "I guess it would be . . . all right. I guess Myron wouldn't . . ."

"I'm sure he wouldn't mind," I told her. "I'm a pretty fair milker, and I'll be careful with your cows."

Without a word, she handed me the buckets and hurried back to the house.

I couldn't be given a straight A for gallantry on my offer to do the milking. I hadn't half filled the cavity inside me with pork and potato, and milk was the only thing on the place that was on my diet list. At most ranches I could have made out with raw eggs, but there wasn't a hen on the Hudson place. As soon as I'd milked a quart from my first cow I drank it, and Paco followed suit. He was a faster milker than I, or got cows that didn't give as much. I'd just started my third when he finished his, stood up, and carried his bucket away toward the gate. There was no reason to hurry, so I pushed my hat back, leaned my forehead against the cow's side, and listened to the rhythmic music of the milk streams. The last strippings were tinkling into the bucket when a quiet voice behind me said, "You're Bud, the one that rode Kitten, ain't you?"

The voice startled me, for I'd never guessed I wasn't alone. But I knew whose voice it would be, and didn't want to show I was startled, so I turned my head slowly, looked up, and said, "Yes, Judy, I'm Bud. And if Kitten is that nice little mare, I'm the one who rode her, why?"

"I reckoned I ought to tell you," she said, "Myron's awful mad at you. Nobody but him has ever rode Kitten before, and he's always swore nobody ever could."

"I don't doubt his swearing," I told her as I rose and moved a step nearer, "but I don't think he's mad at me any more."

Her back was toward the moon, so I couldn't see her face, but she turned it up toward mine and said, "That's 'cause you don't know Myron. He don't forget his mads, and he'll get you . . . one way or another. He gets everybody, sooner or later. He's got Sis tied hand and foot. She wouldn't dast leave him now . . . even if she could."

Judy seemed in no hurry to go, and I didn't want her to. Raising my voice barely enough for Paco to hear, I called him to me, passed him my bucket of milk and, in the best Spanish I could muster, told him to take it to the house, and to wait to turn the separator for the señora.

As he moved away, Judy looked up at me and asked in an awed whisper, "You Mex?"

"No," I told her, "mostly Scotch and English, way back. I learned to talk the lingo a little when I was a kid, working on a cattle ranch in Colorado."

"That where you learned to ride?" she asked.

"Mm-hmm," I said, "but tell me more about Myron. Isn't he a bit cracked in the head?" As I said it I slipped my arm inside hers, and she didn't pull away, so I led her toward the platform where Doc and Paco and I had been sitting when the moon rose.

"Not exactly cracked," she said, "but any more it seems like he's sore at everybody."

I waited till we were seated side by side, then asked, "What's the matter with him? He acted sore at the whole bunch of us before I ever got onto Kitten."

I didn't take my arm out from under Judy's, but let it slip down so that our hands came together, and she didn't take hers away. "Well," she said, "it goes clean back to the time he first come courting Sis, and Paw drove him off . . . told him he wouldn't never amount to nothing 'cause he was rough on stock. Myron, he was working for old man Macey then, got fired the next day. He blamed it onto Paw and told him he'd get even, and he did, too."

"How, Judy?" I asked.

"Getting Sis to run off with him, that's how," she told me. "He had Kitten then; had her when he come riding into Beaver Valley looking for a job. Well, when he got fired he was gone away for a week or two, and when he come back he was leading Vixen, almost a spittin' image of Kitten, only she wasn't mean and ornery. She was the one ought to have been named Kitten —just as clever as a baby kitten. Sis fell in love with Vixen, and run away with Myron to get her. She's been paying for it ever since."

"They couldn't have run far," I said. "Isn't that Beaver Valley where the little town sits at the bottom of the divide?"

"Uh-huh, that's Cedar Bluffs," she said, "where I live in the summertimes. In the winters I go to high school over to Oberlin, and get my keep for doing dishes and minding the baby for a lady. Her husband's in the bank over there, but Myron hates him, 'cause he won't let him have no more money. There won't none of the bankers. That's why he's having to fix that old header now."

As Judy spoke I saw Doc coming down the lane toward us, so when she'd finished I called to him quietly, "Did you find the salt, Doc? I'll be along in a few minutes."

"Okay, Bud," he called back just as quietly, "I'll get some brine ready for those blisters," then he kept straight on.

Judy had half risen when I called to Doc, but I'd drawn her back beside me. As soon as he'd passed she started to rise again, and said, "I'd best go in now. Sis might worry."

I could hear the whine of the separator from the kitchen, so I told her, "Wait till Paco finishes the separating. She won't worry while she's busy with the milk. Besides, you haven't told me yet about her running away with Myron. Was that when they came up here?"

I hadn't sat in the moonlight with a girl for a long, long time, and Judy's hand was soft in mine, so when I drew her back beside me that second time I drew her closer. She didn't really pull away, just ooched over a little, leaving two or three inches between us—and I liked her better for it. She sat for a moment, looking up the golden pathway the moonlight made across the wheat field, then said, "Uh-uh, not up here. This would have been too close to home, and Paw would have come to fetch her back. They run off to the sand hills, up in Nebraska, but Myron didn't do no good up there so they come back . . . right at the beginning of harvest, it was . . . the week before Marthy was born. All they had was Kitten and Vixen . . . and a filly foal out of each one of 'em . . . not even saddles . . . and Sis rode all that ways bareback . . . and her within a week of her time."

There was a catch in her voice as she said the last few words, but it didn't seem right to have any sadness that evening— not there in the moonlight—so to take her mind off her sister I said, "That's a shame, Judy, but you were going to tell me how Myron got the way he is."

"Well, that's when it started," she said, "Paw, he was awful mad, and cussed Myron out, and told him again that he wouldn't never amount to nothing. And Myron cussed Paw back, and told him he'd show him . . . and right under his own nose, too . . . and for a little bit it looked like he was going to do it. Myron ain't lazy. He hired out for a harvest hand to the banker over to Marion . . . that's on the Nebraska side of the line . . . and the banker liked the way he worked, and let him have a quarter section to farm on halvers. It was a good quarter, too, up there on the first bench, but it didn't have no house on it, so Myron put up a little soddy . . . no more'n ten feet square, and him and Sis went down there to live . . . with nothing but a straw bunk and a coal oil stove."

"How could he farm a quarter section with two little ponies like Kitten?" I asked.

"He couldn't," she told me, "and that's when his bad trouble started. The banker left him have money to buy a heavy team and seed wheat, and a secondhanded disk and seeder, and he didn't take no mortgage—only on the next year's crop. But Myron didn't buy no seed, and didn't plant no crop—leastways not on that quarter. That's when he bought Lucy and Lilly, the two bay mares out there in the corral. They were sure a fine team then; Lucy didn't get foundered till that winter— left her stand out when she was sweated up. And he bought two new sets of harness, and a brand new wagon, and disk, and seeder . . . and a couple of cows with heifer calves. Myron was flying high then. Guess he was trying to show Paw and the banker that he was smarter than them. He brought all the stuff across the state line, and mortgaged it to a banker over to Oberlin—the one I mind the baby and wash dishes for his wife when I'm going to school—and he used the mortgage money to pay a year's cash rent for a half section west of The Bluffs, so he wouldn't have to share crop with nobody."

While Judy had been talking I'd heard the separator whir to a stop. Then Paco came out to the corner of the house, stood for a moment or two, and went on toward the barn. I knew Judy should have gone in, but I was interested in her story —and I liked sitting there in the moonlight with her, so I asked, "Didn't the first banker sue Myron and take the crop on the place west of The Bluffs?"

"Oh, he sued him," she said, "but he couldn't get the crop . . . what there was of it. You see, as soon as Myron got the

lease he mortgaged the crop to Bones—he's the banker over
to Cedar Bluffs—to raise money for seed and a couple more
cows and horses."

"Oh," I said, "then that banker got the crop."

"No," she told me, "he didn't, neither. Paw says the Lord
took it away from Myron on account of him trying to be a
thief. Him and Sis—she was proud then, and stout as lots of
men—worked night and day till deep frost come, getting two
hundred and sixty acres of wheat planted. The next spring
they put the other sixty into corn. Wore the horses, all six
of 'em, down to skin and bones. Then, just when the wheat
was making heads, the hail hit 'em. The streak wasn't no more
than half a mile wide and two long, but it beat all their wheat
and most of the corn back into the ground. The rest of it didn't
amount to much . . . just enough to eke 'em through the
winter.

"Bones, he took the two new horses and cows so's to get
something out of his mortgage, and the banker over to Oberlin
took the wagon and disk and seeder. They'd have took the
rest of the stock too, only Lucy was a'ready foundered, the cows
was too thin to sell, and nobody wants ornery little mustangs.
That's when Myron turned sour on everybody. He figured like
they'd tromped on him when he was down, and he's been hunting for somebody to tromp on ever since. There ain't a banker
up or down the valley but he's tangled with, and the both of
'em lose every time."

"Well, if they lose every time how can he keep going?" I
asked.

She hunched her shoulders a particle and said, "By taking
what's left. With wheat as high as it is now the owners will
let anybody take land on shares before leaving it lie fallow,
and no farmer that can get anything else will take land way
up here. Before this one, the last big crop on this divide was
the year Sis and Myron got hailed out. Every year till now
they've had a failure and got kicked off the place they was
on, then had to move higher onto the divide."

For half a minute she sat silently, looking down at our hands, that held us together and yet apart, then said wistfully, "They'd have been rich by now—the war coming on and wheat going up the way it has, and all—if Myron hadn't tried to outsmart the banker over to Marion. That quarter section he put 'em on has raised thirty bushels of wheat to the acre ever since. Their half would have fetched near onto five thousand dollars every year, but Myron, he couldn't be satisfied to be a quarter-section farmer. His trouble is he rares at it too hard, and expects everybody else to . . . and he tries to be smarter'n he is . . . and his word ain't good.

"He's took on more land with every move, as fast as the colts grew big enough to wear harness—they're all out of Kitten and Vixen, her mate that Sis married him for, and that died last winter—and Myron keeps 'em so mean and ornery the bankers daresn't foreclose on 'em. This year he's got two sections in wheat and a quarter in corn. That's why nothing is ready for harvest. Sis has been too poorly this spring to help with the corn, and being a'ready mortgaged to the neck and in trouble with all the bankers, Myron couldn't get a loan to hire help. Working alone, it took him till June to get the last of the corn planted, and with this hot wind coming on he'd have lost it before harvest was over if he didn't get it disk hoed. He finished last night, but that's Myron for you; he always bites off a bigger chunk than he can chew, then blames somebody else if it chokes him."

There were still a few things that puzzled me, so I asked, "If the bankers wouldn't make him a loan for hiring help to put in a hundred and sixty acres of corn, why did they loan him enough for help to plow and seed twelve hundred and eighty acres of wheat? He couldn't have done that alone."

"He didn't, and they didn't," she told me. "There wasn't an acre of it neither plowed nor seeded. Last year's crop was so poor it wasn't worth harvesting, so it was left standing in the fields. That's how Myron got the place. Then him and Sis hogged it back in—you know, disking both ways across it—

and it took 'em till freeze-up to get it done. It's a miracle they got a volunteer crop like this one, and it'll be a bigger miracle if they get it harvested before it shatters or the hail gets it."

She sat silently for a few seconds, just looking off across the moonlit fields, then said, almost in a whisper, "I hope the Lord don't let nothing happen to it. It would be awful hard on Sis and the children. This is the first time they've had better'n a soddy to live in . . . and there ain't no place to move to after you get kicked off the top of the divide."

Although I knew Judy had no idea she was doing it, what she'd really told me was that we'd hired out to a man who didn't have a dime with which to pay our wages, and who was crooked enough that he'd try to beat us out of the money even if he did have it. Of course, I had no way of knowing how big the mortgages and judgments against his crop might be, or if the laws of Kansas would let them stand ahead of wage claims. But that was nothing to worry Judy with. "Don't you worry about it, Judy," I told her. "Unless Myron goes out of his way to pick a fight, and I don't think he will, I'll do all I can to help get this crop harvested, and to keep the crew on the job."

She turned her face toward mine, her eyes warm in the soft light, the breeze stirring a chestnut brown lock that lay across her forehead, and her lips parted slightly as if she were going to speak. When she didn't, I bent my face closer to hers, but she sprang to her feet as if frightened, and there was a touch of tremble in her voice as she told me quickly, "I got to go now . . . Bud. Sis'll be worried." Then she scampered away to the house like a startled quail.

Hudson left the header just as I reached the barn, and when I went around to our camp Gus and Lars were snoring in their tent. Edgar and Everett had spread miscellaneous clothing atop the blackened heap of straw, and were sleeping there, stripped to their B.V.D.'s. Old Bill and Jaikus were wrapped in their blankets, and asleep on their straw mattresses. Paco lay on the naked mattress beside them, still fully dressed, with his sombrero hiding his face from the moonlight. Doc sat apart from the others, dozing, though not asleep. I hadn't made a sound as I came around the barn, but he raised his head and asked, "Conquest?"

"No," I told him, "not even a goodnight kiss. She's a nice little girl, and from what she tells me your guess isn't too far wrong on Hudson, except that he's no drunk."

"Hold it till you get your boots off and your hands and feet soaking in this brine," he told me. "Wheat beards will raise Old Ned with those blisters unless you get 'em hardened up."

It couldn't have hurt much more if I'd stuck my hands and feet into a fire instead of the bucket of brine, but Doc made me keep them there while I told him the story Judy had told me. When I'd finished I said, "You've got to do something to get Hudson out of the way tomorrow night; I'm going to take that little mare and ride to town. I've promised the little girl to stick it out unless he keeps on trying to pick a fight, and that I'd do my best to keep the crew on the job. But there's no sense in our being stuck for our wages, and there's only one way I can think of to head it off. The banker has a mortgage against this crop, but he can't collect unless it's harvested before it shatters. I'm going to put the bee on him to guarantee our wages."

"Now you're whistling!" Doc told me. "When you came back I was sitting here thinking we'd best move on in the morning —soon as we'd had another bait of that delicious pork—but maybe you've got an idea. I'd risk a day's work if I thought it would do that woman and those poor little kids any good— and I'd risk three or four of 'em if I was your age, and a nice little turtle dove would sit in the moonlight and spoon with me. But right now we'd better turn in; we've got a big day ahead tomorrow."

I'd caught a glimpse of Paco when I first came into camp, but had forgotten about him until I was loosening my belt to lie down. Then a pinch came into my throat at the sight of him lying there on the naked heap of straw, his beautiful blanket spread over the larger and deeper pile beside it. He lay

as peacefully as a contented baby, but I couldn't leave him
there while Doc and I went to bed on his blanket, and I was
afraid I might hurt his feelings if I woke him and told him to
move over. I think Doc knew how I felt, and I didn't have to
tell him what I wanted to do. Together we lifted the sleeping
boy carefully and laid him on the center of his blanket. He
didn't wake when we slipped off our overalls and lay down
beside him.

4

Under the Lash

THE moon hung low in the western sky, pale with the breaking of dawn, when Hudson bellowed, "Turn out, all hands of
you!"

I sprang up to one elbow just in time to catch a glimpse of
him turning back from the corner of the barn. Otherwise I'd
have thought I was dreaming, for at that time of year it couldn't
be later than four-thirty, and I'd never heard of a man putting
a crew into the field before seven. For a couple of minutes we
sat on our blankets, grumbling, then pulled on our overalls
and boots, for we had little choice. With the possible exception
of Gus and Lars, every one of us was dead broke.

By the time we'd washed and reached the kitchen, Hudson
was mopping up the grease on his plate with half a biscuit. He
crammed it into his mouth as we sat down, swallowed it almost
whole, and ordered, "Get it into you and come to the corral!"

The breakfast was exactly the same as supper had been, and
there was no sign of Judy or her sister. If it hadn't been for
Hudson's order to get it into us, we'd have stuffed the nauseous
food away as fast as we could, but no one hurried, and no one
looked up from his plate until it was empty. Even at that, we

couldn't have been at the table more than fifteen minutes, and Hudson must have been working at a run.

When we went to the corral the two old bay mares and the four largest mustangs were missing. The six smallest and wildest, together with Kitten, were crowded into the far corner, and two sets of ragged harness lay by the gate. Hudson came out of the barn carrying a third set, dumped it beside the others, and ordered, "Three of you harness the teams in the barn! The rest of you harness these here, exceptin' my saddle mare!" Then he kept right on walking toward the header.

I'd worked on farms and ranches most of my life, and it was always understood that the man who was going to drive a team harnessed it; those who weren't going to drive had no harnessing to do. And whenever there was a new crew the first thing the boss did was to assign each driver the horses he would handle. For maybe a minute we stood there, puzzled, then I noticed that the men were all looking at me, but I was as puzzled as they were. There were only two drivers among us—Old Bill and Doc—but there were three barges, three pairs of pitchers, and twelve horses.

There was no doubt that harnessing the wild bunch was going to be up to me, so I looked around the circle to see who might be able to help me. I knew Gus and Lars would be too slow, so when I caught their eyes I nodded toward the barn, then nodded for Doc to go with them. Edgar and Everett looked plain scared, and Jaikus beat me to the punch. "Don't be lookin' at me," he jabbered in his thick brogue, "I come here to pitch wheat, not to be fightin' divils."

Only Paco looked straight at me, and his eyes were bright with excitement. "Go find a throw rope and a long piece of baling wire," I told him, "and say a prayer before you bring them back." Then I told the others, "Come in and give us a hand at holding the horses in the corner, but keep clear of their teeth and heels, and watch yourselves. Each of you bring a bridle."

Edgar, Everett, and Jaikus stayed out of the corral, but Old

Bill followed me without the slightest show of fear. He was cautious, but spry as a cat, and was always in the right spot to head a horse back when it tried to break from the corner.

When Paco came back, white teeth flashing and eyes dancing, I knew he was a natural horseman—far beyond my ability—that he'd tackled many a mean bronco, and liked nothing better. The rope he'd found was a worn old piece of half-inch, not more than fifteen feet long, but he'd already tied a honda at the end, and was drawing a three-foot loop through it. He held the rope out to me as we crossed the corral toward the frightened, milling horses, but I shook my head and told him, "No, you throw it."

With six feet of the rope doubled into the loop, a man had to get dangerously close to those flying heels to make a catch, but Paco darted in and out like a terrier worrying a pack of fighting rats. He didn't try to swing the clumsy rope, but held the loop behind one hip, and flipped it overhand to catch the first head that turned toward him. Then the fight was on. With both of us hanging to the rope and digging our heels in, the little seven-hundred-pound mustang dragged us half the length of the corral, rearing and bucking, before we could get her snubbed to a post. We'd no sooner snubbed her than Paco snatched a wire from his belt and, dodging her striking hoofs, slipped a loop around her muzzle. There was no need of tightening the loop; she knew the pain it could cause only too well, and stood trembling while I harnessed her.

Each of the six frightened little horses handled in about the same way, though a couple of them gave us a harder battle than the others. I'd expected the harnessing to take us more than an hour, but with Paco's skill and cunning it was less than half that time until we had them lined up, one at each corral post. When I went to the barn, Lars was buckling the last straps on a fractious gelding, and the other five were already harnessed. As I stood watching for a minute, Gus told me, "Goot little horses; yust spoilt rotten." Except for their names, it was the first thing I'd heard either him or Lars say.

I'd paid no attention to Hudson while we'd been harnessing, but he'd evidently been watching us closely enough to know we were finished. He came storming into the barn just as Gus told me the horses were spoiled rotten, and could hardly have helped hearing it. He was almost on the run, and kept right on past us to the far end of the barn, but as he went he shouted, "Don't be loafin' around in here! Get them horses hitched onto the barges!"

At the sound of Hudson's voice the four mustangs panicked, crowding into the farthest corners of the stalls as if they'd been trying to hide. It would have been senseless and dangerous to rush into those stalls, so I motioned Doc and Gus to stay back. After the horses had quieted a bit I went into the nearest stall, and was just reaching for a halter buckle when Hudson threw them into another panic. "Get 'em out of here!" he shouted. "Get 'em out of here! I ain't got all day to waste!"

I had to duck for cover as he passed the back of the stall, a bundle of sticks about three feet long under an arm, and trailing a blacksnake whip about half as long as the one he'd used for cutting the horses the night before.

The old bay mares had either become used to Hudson's shouting, or he'd treated them less roughly than the mustangs. He'd barely left the barn before Doc led them out, and a minute later Gus followed with the second team, but it was two or three before my pair quieted enough that I could back them out of the stall.

As I led my fractious team to the water tank I had a chance to figure out several things I should have noticed earlier. The pair Gus had led out were much heavier than mine, and were far less wild. It was evident that Hudson had been using them and the old mares for working his corn crop, so they were fairly well worked down. My team must have been a spare, used only once in a while, and the six in the corral hadn't probably been in from pasture since the previous fall. While we'd been catching and harnessing the wild bunch I'd seen enough of Old Bill to know he was no stranger to horses, but

I couldn't be too sure of Doc, so while my team was drinking I nodded to Bill and he came to me. "Why don't you take this team?" I asked him quietly. "They're going to take some handling the first day or two, and I'm afraid Doc might have a little trouble with them."

Old Bill couldn't have been more pleased if I'd slipped him a twenty-dollar goldpiece. He peeked up at me from under the visor of his cap, grinned, and told me, "I'll handle 'em, Bud. Just give me a hand a-gettin' 'em hooked to the barge the first time. Always did like a team with a little get-up-and-go to it."

As soon as Bill's team was hitched to a barge I went to the corral, where Hudson had the six little broncos lined up in two teams of three each, with the two wildest in the centers. Each team was poled together with the sticks he'd brought from the barn, one end wired to a hame, and the other to a bit ring on the next horse's bridle. With the sticks crossed in X's between each pair, no horse in a team could rear, crowd, or pull aside more than an inch or two without tearing its mouth. Paco was helping Hudson put jerk lines on one of the teams when I swung the gate back to go into the corral, but Hudson shouted to me, "Leave that gate open and take this team out! This Mex can't talk American."

Those little horses knew the punishment of jockey poles too well to fight them, and I had no trouble in driving when I picked up the jerk lines. Hudson led the way with the other team, trailing his blacksnake behind him. Although the horses had stood all night without water, he didn't let them go to the tank, but yanked them around and drove them to the header. The only trouble we had in hooking them to it was in being careful to avoid a flying heel or two. I'd lost all track of time during the harnessing, and when I stepped back from hooking the last trace chain I was surprised to see that the sun was only an hour high. I'd also forgotten that we were short one driver until Hudson turned toward the house, and yelled, "Hey, you! Get out here!"

Hudson's voice had barely echoed back before Judy came

around the corner from the kitchen. She had on a faded denim jacket that must have been her sister's, and pulled up over it was a pair of overalls that must have been Hudson's. The shoulder straps had been shortened until the bib reached nearly to her chin, and a foot or more of the legs was folded into cuffs. With her hair tucked inside a big cap that pulled down over her ears, she looked like a teddy bear as she came running toward the first barge in the line, the one with the two old mares hitched to it. Edgar and Everett headed for it too, but Hudson bawled at them, "Get outa there and take that barge where the Swedes are at!" That left Paco and Jaikus to go as Old Bill's pitchers. And since I'd hired out to do the stacking I just picked up a pitchfork and stood off to one side—anxious to see how a header worked, and how Hudson was going to steer it and handle all the levers and pulleys while driving two teams of half-wild mustangs.

Astraddle of the rudder bar, and perched, nearly standing, on the little seat at the top of the steering post, he hung each pair of jerk lines around his neck, then pulled down the boom that lifted the cutting machinery. As it rose, not more than two or three feet in front of the already frightened horses' heads, they went into a panic, fear of the monster rising toward them greater than their fear of the punishing jockey poles wired to their bits. Dancing, plunging, and rearing till the poles jerked them down, each team swung outward, trying to escape the awesome contraption, but Hudson yanked the inside jerk lines with all his tremendous strength. At the same time he swung his whip from side to side, lashing the outside horses on their faces and driving them inward.

Whether intentionally or through carelessness, Hudson had left the machine in gear. As the horses plunged away from the sting of his whip they lurched forward into their collars, turning the drive wheel and setting the clattering cutter bar, the reel, and the conveyor belts into motion. Insane with fright the horses leaped back, but Hudson poured the blacksnake across their backs until the welts gave them the appearance

of zebras, driving them inward and forward toward the clattering, whirling-armed monster before them.

From the time I'd talked with Judy I'd promised myself that
I wouldn't let Hudson goad me into losing my temper and
starting any further trouble between us. I don't believe he
could have done it by any amount of yelling and swearing at
me, but to stand there watching him beat those defenseless
horses, and yank the jerk lines till their mouths bled, drove me
nearly as insane as they were. Before I realized what I was
doing I ran toward him with the pitchfork raised above my
head, shouting, "Lay off those horses, you coward!"

I suppose I'd have tried to knock the whip out of his hands
if I'd got close enough, but I didn't—and he did the knocking.
I was still three good long strides away when the whip lashed
out in my direction, and the fork went flying from my hands
as if it had been struck by lightning. As the fork sailed away
he shouted, "Keep outa this, you fool!"

Doc and Paco must have started running the instant I did, and they grabbed me before I could prove that Hudson had been right in what he called me. Their grabbing brought me to my senses, but it didn't do my judgment much good.

"Let's get out of here, Bud," Doc told me as he pinned my arms back. "There's nothing you can do to stop him, and he'll kill you if he takes after you with that whip."

"Don't worry about that whip," I told Doc, "he'll never touch me with it. He's had two chances now, and he didn't dare do it either time. You quit if you want to, but I'm going to stay right here till I get those horses away from him. I don't know how I'll do it, but I will."

I really did the horses more harm than if I'd kept my head and held my tongue. For three or four minutes Hudson took his anger at me out on them, lashing them, driving them ahead a few feet, then yanking them to a stop. Shouting, swearing, whipping, and yanking the jerk lines, he put the horses through a drill until they could make a square turn without moving the machine either forward or back. When, at last, he was satisfied with the turns, he threw the machine out of gear, drove toward the roadway, and motioned for Judy to follow with the front barge in the waiting line. She didn't turn her head toward me as she passed, but she did turn her eyes, and her voice was barely loud enough for me to hear when she said, "You watch out for him, Bud. He hates you enough a'ready."

"I'll watch him," I told her just as quietly, then hopped onto Old Bill's barge as it passed. His team was rearing and dancing, but he seemed to pay no attention to their plunging. The first thing I noticed was his hands. He held the reins just firmly enough to keep a steady, restraining pressure on the bit, but not enough to anger or annoy the broncs. I needed no one to tell me that he was an expert horseman, one who had been handling high-strung horses for more years than I'd lived, so I asked, "Where did you develop those rein hands, Bill?"

"Exercisin' trotters," he told me. "Spent all my life around the race tracks and stables, but work's been slack since the war. An old rooster like me has to take any job he can get."

Old Bill's handling of his horses not only quieted them, but quieted the anger that was still boiling inside me. I paid no more attention to Hudson until I heard him yell, "Keep your head about you and watch what you're doin'! Back that team up and pull in where you belong!"

Hudson had turned the header so that it faced the edge of the wheat field, and Judy had turned her barge to bring it under the conveyor elevator. I looked up just in time to see Gus and Lars start across the floor of the barge toward Hudson, pitchforks in hand. Neither of them made a sound, but there was something in the way they moved that made me catch my breath. I think it made Hudson catch his, too. His whip lashed out across his horses' backs, and they leaped into their collars, sending the header ripping into the wheat field with a rush.

Hudson grabbed frantically for the boom, the gear lever, and the pulley ropes. But the horses had started with such a rush that the header was dragged more than a hundred feet, ripping the dead-ripe grain to the ground, before he could set the machinery in motion and lower the elevator enough that the conveyor belt could carry the cut grain up into the barge. Long before it got there Judy had the barge in position to catch it, but the only way she could keep it there was by beating the slow old mares with the rein ends, forcing them into a lumbering trot.

Old Bill turned in behind the header, and I became convinced that Hudson was actually insane or on the verge of insanity. With a worn-out old header, a girl driving the barge, and six frightened mustangs to handle, he kept his whip flailing and his horses at as near a trot as they could pull the heavy machine. The swath he cut through that field was far from straight, but only a man with tremendous strength could have held any line at all. Wheat poured off the end of the conveyor belt like water rushing through a floodgate, and to keep the barge under the weaving stream, Judy had to drive with her `head turned back, flogging the old mares and pulling them from side to side. By the time Hudson had cut a swath a quarter-mile into the field the barge was heaped to overflowing. He pulled his horses to a stop, made a right angle turn, and shouted, "Next barge! Stackyard here!"

I jumped off Bill's barge, and he brought it squarely under the elevator just as Hudson finished his turn. His coming in so smoothly seemed to anger Hudson. He lashed his horses and sent the header into the new swath like a wriggling snake, crashing the elevator against the side of the barge, then veering it out far enough to throw the cut grain onto the ground. And with each erratic veer he bawled at Bill to watch what he was doing and keep the barge under the elevator.

I never saw any man take the play away from another so quickly and completely. Old Bill never once looked back at the crazily lurching elevator, or paid the slightest attention to Hudson, but set a course as straight as a taut string, forcing Hudson to fight the rudder and quit flogging his horses in order to keep the stream of wheat flowing into the barge. He cut three short swaths down the field and back to make room for the stackyard, then yelled for Doc's barge—and my troubles began.

With Doc's barge under the elevator, Hudson kept straight on toward the far end of the field, a quarter-mile away, and again whipped his horses nearly to a trot. Gus and Lars were evidently afraid Judy would have trouble in catching up to take her turn, and they nearly buried me. Plunging their forks nearly to the floor boards, they heaved, and rolled about half the load off over the low side of the barge. Before I could more than get my fork into it, they'd sent the other half of the load tumbling down, burying me to the waist. They didn't bother to clean out the barge, but scooped off the bulk of what was left with a few swipes of their forks, and before I could paw my way out of the mess Judy had larruped the old mares into a trot and was halfway out of the stackyard.

Fortunately, Jaikus and Paco weren't as strong as Gus and

Lars, but they scooped wheat out of there fast enough that I couldn't do much beside dodge the forkfuls. Then Old Bill drove away at a trot, and across the quarter-mile-square field I could see Judy pulling her barge in beside the header while Doc turned back with a heaping load.

It was then I discovered that I didn't know any more about stacking wheat than a goose knows about knitting mittens. It didn't handle like hay, wouldn't bind together in good fork- fuls, and was as slippery as wet spaghetti. I had to get the heap spread out into some semblance of a stack before any more was piled onto it, and the only way I could think of do- ing it was by getting on top and scooping as fast and far as I could in both directions. I was so winded I couldn't speak when Doc pulled his load alongside, and my stack looked like something that had been left over from a hurricane. There were only two things that saved me: Doc and the greenness of Edgar and Everett.

The boys held their pitchforks as if they were long-handled soup spoons, and with each dab they made at the load they pushed off about as much wheat as a fellow could stuff in his hat. I didn't stop to look up at them, but kept flailing away with my own fork until Doc caught my eye and motioned me to him. "You're going at it all wrong, Bud," he told me quietly. "I'd trade jobs with you only I got my belly full of wheat stack- ing when I was a kid, and promised myself I'd never do an- other day's work that would put callouses on my hands. Don't try to pitch it like hay. Turn your fork over and use it like you were sweeping deep sand with a broom. Then push it to the outside, but don't try to tread too close to the edge; it would slip out like hot mush. I'll let you know how your sides are building; don't worry too much about 'em. Make your stack about thirty feet long and fifteen wide, and let it round up a little in the middle. Now take it easy; there's no sense in killing yourself off for this wild man. That's what he's trying to do to the whole bunch of us, horses and all. He's taking twice as much straw as there's any need for, just to pour the work onto us."

I ripped into the heap and dragged wheat, as Doc told me where to push it and how to handle it. By the time Judy turned into the yard with her load I had the heap squared out enough that it looked like the beginning of a stack, but the boys weren't half finished with their unloading. As Judy pulled in behind Doc's barge, I heard Hudson yell, "Get that barge unloaded and back here! Driver, give them kids a hand!"

I'd been too busy to pay any attention to Hudson, but had an idea he was still at the far end of the field, and was surprised to hear his voice so plainly. When I looked up I found that he had nearly circled the field. The header was standing no more than a couple of hundred yards away, and Old Bill was pulling away from it with his barge loaded high. I'd barely glanced up when Doc shouted back, "No business! I hired out as a driver!"

Doc had no sooner refused than Hudson shouted, "One of you Swedes trade places with one of them kids! I don't aim to pay for no time when this header ain't rollin'!"

For maybe ten seconds Gus and Lars mumbled to each other, then started to climb down from the barge, and Lars told Judy, "Ve kvit."

She caught her breath sharply as he said it, and when I looked up two big tears were brimming in her eyes. I knew well enough why they were there, and I'd promised her I'd do everything I could to keep the crew on the job, so I asked Gus and Lars to wait a minute, then went to the barge. I told them in the simplest words I could find that they could have my day's pay if they'd stay and each work with one of the boys. They mumbled a few more words in Swedish, then Lars nodded and went to climb on Doc's barge.

The rest of the forenoon was a series of mad rushes and stops. Hudson drove at the job as if he were trying to harvest the whole two sections in a single day, but the conveyor belts on the header, probably eight or ten years old, couldn't stand the strain. With the crop having sprung from volunteer seeding, it wasn't evenly spread over the land. In some places it was thin, but in others thick and rank. Any reasonable man would have kept his horses at a slow walk, and would have raised or lowered his cutter bar so as to take only the heads and three or four inches of straw, but Hudson set his cutter low enough to catch the shortest heads and left it there, putting a terrific strain on the horses and the worn-out old header. Half a dozen times the conveyor belt broke from being overloaded, and each time it took Hudson nearly half an hour to repair it.

The breakdowns were lifesavers for the horses and me, for they gave me time to square my stack into shape, but they were rough on Edgar and Everett. They were the only ones Hudson dared vent his anger on, and from clear across the field I could hear him yelling and swearing at them. I have an idea they had promised each other to finish out the day in spite of anything, but if so Everett broke his promise. At about eleven o'clock, he blew sky high, jumped off the barge with his pitchfork held in both hands, and for a second or two I thought he was going to rush Hudson with it, but he stopped just beyond reach of the whip, shouting that they'd quit and demanded their wages right then. Hudson roared back that they hadn't earned the grub they'd eaten, then whipped up his horses and drove on.

The boys followed the header for a few yards, shouting that they'd have their attorney take care of Hudson, then they gave up and limped toward the house. Just before we knocked off for noon I saw them hobbling toward the main road, carrying their suitcases and looking as dejected as any pair of boys I'd ever seen. Their leaving was more or less a relief to the rest of us. As far as Gus and Lars were concerned, they'd only been in the way, and as soon as they were gone Hudson cooled down a little, probably convinced that Gus and Lars would go right on doing double work, and that he'd saved himself fourteen dollars a day. Then too, as the horses began to tire he couldn't keep them at so fast a pace, so the header gave less trouble.

By noon the temperature was above 110°, I was sweating so much that the wheat beards stuck to my back and belly like a swarm of stinging mosquitoes, and the blisters on both hands had broken. Each time Doc came in with a load he scolded at me for going at my job too hard, and told me the easier ways to do it, but I couldn't pick up the knack well enough to find a minute's rest without letting my stack get out of shape. Then too, I'd run out of breakfast long before Hudson shouted, "Grub!" from the far end of the field.

I rode in from the stack with Judy and Gus, and when we reached the corral Hudson was nowhere in sight. He'd left the header in the middle of the yard, and Paco was unhooking the trace chains. Doc and Bill were unhitching their own teams, and Jaikus was pitching a little dab of wheat into the corral from one of the barges. Judy would have gone right to work at unhitching her team, but I told her to run along, and Gus did the unhitching while I helped Paco with the header teams. All the horses were dripping with sweat, so we didn't dare let them have much water, but gave each one a dozen swallows or so before putting them into the corral to make out a meal on that dry, bearded wheat straw. When we stripped off their bridles no one would have guessed they were the same broncos we'd harnessed that morning. They were so worked-down and starved that all the fight had gone out of them.

The children were playing near the windmill when we left the corral to wash up for dinner. They stood watching us until we were halfway to them—half curious, half frightened, like four little antelopes—then ran away behind the house. We'd washed and were just starting for the kitchen when Hudson came out. He avoided looking our way, and hurried off toward the header.

Dinner was on the table when we went in—exactly the same things we'd had for supper and breakfast—and Judy was clearing away Hudson's dirty dishes. She looked up and smiled, started to say something, then stopped with her lips pinched tightly together as if she were having to hold it back. After she'd put on a clean plate and cup she sat down and helped herself to a potato, a biscuit, and some gravy, but she just shook

her head when I passed her the platter of boar pork. The other
fellows ate it for the same reason I did, but there was hardly
a word said during the meal.

We stuffed in as much of the nauseating grub as we could
stomach, left the table, and went out to sit in the narrow strip
of shade on the north side of the house, glad of the half hour's
rest before it would be time to go back to the field. Hudson
was at the header, hammering rivets into the spliced old conveyor belt, and barely let us sit down before he yelled, "Get
them horses hitched up! What you loafin' there fore? I've lost
time enough a'ready!"

When Hudson yelled the other fellows all looked toward me,
so I said, "Let's do it. If we'd quit now we wouldn't come out
any better than the boys did, and maybe I can get things
straightened out by morning. If not, we'll quit then. Is that fair
enough?" No one answered, but they all got to their feet.

No matter how tough a decent farmer may be with his hired
help, he'll give his horses a full hour's rest at noon. And even
though he may be stingy in the table he sets, he'll see that his
horses are well fed and watered. The amount of feed Hudson
had sent in from the field wasn't more than half enough for
thirteen horses, and they were fighting each other away from
the last few straws when we went to the corral for them.

The afternoon went a little better for the fellows on the
barges, but worse than ever for the horses—and it wasn't too
easy for me. I don't know how hot it might have been that
afternoon, but well above 110°, and there wasn't a breath of
air stirring. Fortunately, the drivers carried water jugs, wrapped
in a wet sack and hung under the barge. Each time a load came
in I must have drunk a pint. I sweated it out almost as fast as
I drank it, and the more I sweat the more stinging beards
stuck to my skin.

Hudson didn't waste any time yelling at the barge crews,
and they didn't give him anything he could yell about. Their
job, like mine, grew harder as the stack grew taller, but Hudson
never had to wait one minute for an empty barge. And except

for a few breakdowns, he didn't wait for anything else. Even if he'd had well-seasoned horses, heavy enough for the oversized header, the pace he was setting would have been nearly enough to kill them. For the ones he was driving it was nothing short of torture, and as they began to slow down he poured the black-snake onto their backs. By mid-afternoon every horse in the header teams had zebra stripes, but they'd reached the point where they didn't even jump when the whip hit them, and with each round I noticed that they'd slowed their pace a bit more.

As the sun sunk lower all the spirit drained out of Hudson's horses. They plodded along like benumbed, half-frozen cattle in a blizzard, too exhausted to pay the least attention to the whip. That was probably all that saved the pitchers and me from keeling over in the heat, for as the horses slowed it gave us time to catch a couple of minute's rest between each load.

I don't believe there were a dozen words spoken between the crew that afternoon, except, "Pass the jug, will you?" We'd all made up our minds to see the day through, and we were doing it just about as the header horses were. The sun was just setting, so it must have been about half-past-seven, when Hudson finished the last swath of the quarter-mile-square field, then without a word he turned the header toward the house.

Doc's barge was the last one in from the field, so we left about a foot of wheat on the floor for horse feed. He pulled in close to the corral fence, and as he and I jumped down to un-hook the traces Lars began pitching the horses' supper over the fence. He'd pitched only three or four forkfuls when Hudson came out of the barn, shouting, "Don't pitch that in there! Turn them horses out to pasture!" Then he kept straight on to the house.

With it being Saturday night, I could only think that Hudson was going to lay off for Sunday, though few farmers did in harvest time. Even if the horses were going to have a day's rest, I couldn't imagine any man in his right mind turning them out to pasture without a feeding of grain, but there was nothing we could do except to follow his orders or quit.

It was dusk by the time we'd unharnessed and turned the horses out to pasture, and a lamp was lighted in the kitchen when we went to the windmill to wash up for supper. I wasn't surprised when Hudson came out and hurried away toward the barn. It was a relief, as tired as we were, that we wouldn't have to eat at the same table with him.

Supper—exactly like the other meals—was on the table, and eight places were set, with Hudson's dirty dishes at one of them. Beyond the half-closed door to the next room a child whimpered, but there was no other sound. We'd barely taken our places when I heard the engine of the old Maxwell roar and backfire. There was a clashing of gears, then the sound of the engine grew fainter and farther away. As before, we ate in silence and left the table as soon as we'd finished. I was too tired to be hungry, but fiddled along so as to be the last to leave. At the doorway I stopped and called quietly, "Judy."

She came from the other room as quickly as if she'd been waiting for my call, and there was a half-embarrassed, half-frightened look on her face. She didn't speak until she'd crossed the kitchen and was within a foot or two of me, then she looked up and said huskily, "Bud, I'm sorry, and I'm ashamed, but . . ."

Although I'd had no intention of doing it, I stepped closer and put an arm around her shoulders. "Neither you nor your sister has anything to be sorry for or ashamed of," I told her, "so stop your worrying. We're not going to quit tonight, and maybe we're not going to quit at all, but I've got to know where Myron has gone and how long he may be away."

She turned her face up to me and said, "To Oberlin, to try and get new conveyor belts, and without he has good luck he'll prob'ly be late. Why do you need to know, Bud?"

"Because I'm going to take Kitten and ride in to see the banker at The Bluffs," I told her.

She caught a quick, sharp breath, and there was a tinge of terror in her voice when she whispered, "No, Bud! No, you

can't! She'd kill you! Myron's learned her to be as dirty and
sneakin' as he is. She's come near to killing three men a'ready,
and there ain't nobody rode her till you did yesterday . . .
nobody but Myron, and the only way he can do it is by keeping her scairt of him."

As I turned to go I told her, "I'll watch her, Judy, but I've
got to take her. If I don't see that banker tonight—and have
some luck with him—there won't be any crew here tomorrow
morning. Paco'll take care of the milking."

5

Banker Bones

WHEN I left the kitchen, after telling Judy I was going to see the banker, the rest of the crew was waiting for me. "You still aiming to ride into town tonight?" Doc asked.

"Right away," I told him. "I've had a couple more ideas during the day, and if I can't sell them to that banker we'll get out of here in the morning. I'm not going to stick around to see those horses killed, much as I'd like to help the woman and those little kids."

"That's two of us," Doc said. "Want me to bring the saddle?"

"No," I said, "I don't dare risk it. Not that I'm hankering for any more blisters on my tail end, but that little mare flips over awful fast, and I don't want to be caught in any saddle gear if she does it. You fellows turn in. I'll be back as soon as I can."

In the starlight I could see Kitten at the far side of the corral when I went in, so I stopped, talking quietly, to let her catch my scent. Horses, particularly mustangs, can tell whether or not a man is afraid by the smell of him, and I think they can tell a lot more: Whether he is angry, irritable, rough, or gentle. I waited a minute or two, mumbling small talk, then snapped one rein above my head. Instantly, Kitten whirled and stood facing me. I had to gamble on whether she'd remember me with hatred or willingness to let me ride her, so I walked straight to her as if I knew her to be the gentlest horse on earth—and she stood for bridling as if she were. I led her out of the corral, watered her, slipped the reins around her neck, and flipped aboard, ready to jump for my life if she reared. She didn't, but swung into an easy rhythmic lope that any child could have ridden. The ride to town must have taken more than a half hour, but it seemed less, for I had to do some careful thinking on the way.

Even though it was Saturday night I was surprised to find the bank and stores open. A dozen or more teams were tied up at hitch rails, and nearly as many flivvers were parked along the main street. I left Kitten at the rail in front of the bank, rehearsed my opening speech quickly in my mind, and went in.

The little bank was divided T shaped, with a few feet of customers' space at the front. Beyond, a cashier's cage filled one side of the room, and the other was the banker's office, cut off from the customers' space by a railing with a closed gate in it. There were three or four ranchers lined up at the cashier's window, and at the back of the office space a man sat working at an old roll-topped desk. He looked to be in his middle fifties, had sparse reddish hair, and was a little less than medium in size. He wasn't particularly thin, but had the craggiest face I'd ever seen on a small man; brow, cheek, jaw, and temple bones standing out sharply. I knew he'd be the man Judy called Bones.

I stood at the gate two or three minutes, and cleared my throat loudly, but the banker didn't look up from his desk, so I opened the gate and went in. He let me reach his desk before he looked up, fixed me with bright blue eyes, and demanded, "Well? What do you want?"

With that kind of a start, the opening speech I'd planned wouldn't have been worth a dime, so I said, "To help you and have you help me."

"I don't need any help," he told me brusquely, "and I don't make loans without security."

"But sometimes security doesn't do a banker much good, does it?" I said. "If I understand right, you have a lien on at least a part of Myron Hudson's wheat crop, and a mortgage on everything else he has. I think I'm the only man who can do you much good in getting your money back."

Bones had never moved his eyes from mine, but neither they nor his voice were so sharp when he said, "I never talk business with strangers. Who are you? Who's your father?"

I told him my name, that my father wasn't living, that my mother and our family now lived in Massachusetts, but that I had been sent back West because of my health, and that I was one of Hudson's harvest crew. When I'd finished he leaned back in his chair and said, "Sit down, Son. What's on your mind?"

I sat down beside the desk and told him, "I don't know whether or not the man is crazy, but from the way he went at things today he might as well be. If he abuses his horses just one more day as he did today he'll break them down or kill them, and if I can't take back some assurance from you he won't have a man on the place by morning. What's more, he can only hire men in McCook, where they won't be tipped off before they hire out to him, and even if he hires them he won't be able to hold them more than a day—not if he feeds and treats them as he's fed and treated us. And without horses and a crew he'll never get that crop harvested before it shatters onto the ground."

When I'd finished Bones sat for a minute or two, rocking back and forth in his swivel chair, and evidently trying to figure out what I was leading up to. "Well," he said at last, "if he's crazy, he's crazy like a weasel . . . and slippery as a wet frog . . . has been ever since he came into this country. I know how he treats his stock and his help . . . if he's lucky enough to catch any. Treats us bankers the same way when he catches us, and he's caught most of us, one way or another.

"Sure, we all hold liens against his crop, and you're right as rain about the chance of getting it harvested, but what can we do about it? We can't go out there and make him behave, and there's no sense hauling him into court any more. Sue a beggar and catch a louse. Catch a weasel and he'll do you more hurt than if you leave him alone. Afraid I can't do much for you, Son. The only chance we bankers have is to play along with him now that he's got a crop, round up a new crew for him every day if we have to, and hope those little nags of his will hold out till he gets enough wheat harvested that it'll be worth attaching."

"I don't think so," I said. "You're holding the mortgage on his horses and equipment, aren't you?"

He looked at me, half-irritated, half-puzzled, and said, "Sure. Sure, I hold a mortgage on everything out there, but what good is that going to do? All he's got is a bunch of junk that wouldn't bring a hundred dollars. You talk about horses; he hasn't got any. Nothing but a herd of wild little broncos that everybody knows are as crazy as Hudson himself. A man couldn't get ten dollars apiece for 'em! Not if he was to throw in the halter and harness! Take them away from him and what chance would there be of getting an acre of that crop harvested?"

"Plenty," I said. "That's what I came to talk to you about."

He sat for at least a minute, just looking straight into my eyes. Then he said, "Well?"

"I want to buy all that equipment, harness, and every horse and colt on the place. You foreclose on it, and I'll take it off your hands at three hundred dollars. I haven't got a dime, but I'll sign a note for it, payable on the first of August."

By the time I'd gone that far Bones was shaking his head vigorously, but I kept right on. "Then I'll make all you bankers who hold liens on that crop a proposition," I told him. "For two dollars an acre I'll harvest the whole two sections and have it in the stacks by the end of July. I can keep the present crew, will feed it, and hire whatever extra help and equipment is necessary to get the job done by the end of the month. At any time I fall more than two days behind schedule you bankers can cancel the deal by paying me a dollar and a half an acre for whatever we've harvested up to that time. The other fifty cents an acre is to be credited against my note for the horses and equipment. What's more, I'll sign a note you can foreclose without going to court if the contract is cancelled before six hundred acres are harvested."

Bones stopped shaking his head, but looked at me as if I were some sort of a curious animal in a zoo. I just grinned at him and said, "There are still a couple of hookers to the proposition. I told you I didn't have a dime, so I'll need something to come and go on. I want a line of credit at one of the stores here in town; enough to cover grub, whatever clothes the crew may need, and repair parts for harness and equipment. Then I want you to open an account for me here in the bank and credit it with eighty dollars for the forty acres we harvested today. After that you can check on us each week, and credit the account for whatever acreage we've put into the stacks."

Scowling at me, he asked, "Where does the rest of the crew get off if I credit it all to you?"

"They trust me," I told him. "Check with them if you'd like to."

Bones looked at me sharply for another minute, then stuck out his hand and said, "So do I, Son. You've made a deal. But you understand there's nothing can be done about it before Monday. Tomorrow I'll get in touch with the other lien holders—they'll go along all right—but we'll have to go before a judge to get attachments, and the sheriff will have to serve them before. . . . Say, what do you aim to do about Hudson? He'll be a wild man when those attachments are served on him. He'll get you any way he can, and he's clever at it. Do you think you're big enough to stand him off. A sheriff can't stay there to protect you."

"I'd thought of that," I said, "but I'm not afraid of him. In the first place he's a coward, and in the second place the whole crew is itching to lay hands on him. I won't do anything about him if he leaves us and the horses alone. If he doesn't I'll swear out a warrant and have him thrown in the calaboose till the job is finished."

"Sure, you could have him arrested and held if you could get proof against him," Bones told me. "The sheriff's kind of like your crew; itching to lay hands on Hudson, but like I told you, he's slippery as a wet frog. If he gets wind you're behind this he'll get you when you're alone, someplace where there won't be any witnesses around, then whip the whey out of you. That's the way he does it, then claims self-defense, and it's one man's word against another's. You can't throw a man in the calaboose till you prove him guilty. I'm afraid you're trying to bite off a bigger wad than you can chew."

"I'll risk it if you will," I told him. "He'll never lay a hand on me—or a whip either. He had his chance when we were alone, and when he was mad enough to kill me, but he didn't dare risk it. He never will. How about our deal; have we got one?"

Instead of answering, Bones stuck out his hand and shook with me again, so I asked, "Will you write me out a memorandum; something to show the other fellows?"

"Fair enough," he said, then turned to his desk and scribbled a few words on the back of a blank check. As he passed it to me he said, "That's to Joe, in the store this side of the street. He'll let you have what you need, but don't go to laying in any groceries yet awhile. You boys will have to make out the best you can till Monday, and you'll have to keep mum, but I'll write you out a memo while you're getting your stuff. It'll be ready by the time you come back."

In a hand clear enough that I could read it at a glance, Bones had written, "Joe—Give this boy what he wants—up to $50. I'll stand good for it."

I'd planned to get a few cans of salmon, so I could stay somewhere near my diet, but after what the banker had said about groceries I thought I'd better not. Instead, I picked out the things Doc and I needed most: a pair of wool blankets, overalls, blue shirts, good solid work shoes, and horsehide gloves. I rolled the stuff in the blankets, tied them into a shoulder sling, and went back to the bank.

Bones had the memorandum ready for me, written in indelible pencil, with a carbon copy. It was short, but covered the deal just the way I'd laid it out, although Hudson's name was never mentioned. The last sentence was: "This agreement to become effective only in the event that, not later than July 10, 1919, certain writs of attachment discussed by the parties hereto shall have been granted by judicial authority."

We both knew the paper was nothing more than an unenforceable memorandum. When I'd read it I signed the original and slid it over on Bones' desk. Then he signed the duplicate, passed it to me, and held out his hand, as much as to say, "This paper is worthless, but here's my hand on the deal."

As we shook he looked me straight in the eyes, and said, "You understand, Son, I can only speak for myself right now. I'll go through with the mortgage foreclosure on the horses and other stuff for you, but I won't guarantee the rest of the deal unless the other lien holders stand with me and we get a court order. I'll do the best I can, and they'll just about have to go along. If they do, we'll try to get the attachments on Monday, but till we get 'em you boys will have to make out the best you can."

"We couldn't ask for anything more," I told him, "and we'll gamble on our wages up to the tenth." Then I grinned and added, "Of course, you understand I'm talking only for myself right now, but I think the rest of the crew will go along."

Bones slapped me on the back, and said, "I'll bet on you, Son. If you haven't heard from me by Monday evening, come see me. My house is right across the corner."

Kitten spooked when I went toward her with the blanket roll across my shoulder. I had to waste maybe ten minutes, letting her look it over and smell it before she quieted enough to be mounted. Then I held her to a walk until we'd climbed the high hills that rimmed the valley. There I let her out to a lope, but slowed her at each deep gulch or steep hill, for I'd blistered badly from so long a bareback ride.

We'd reached the top of the divide and picked up the lope again when headlights came into sight about a mile ahead of us. A minute or so later they turned off to the east, and I knew whose lights they were. I slowed Kitten to a walk, and watched the lights turn down between the wheat fields, then describe a small circle in the yard and blink out. A few minutes later a tiny oblong of yellow light showed that a lamp had been lighted in the house. I stopped Kitten, and she stood quietly until the light went out. Then I rode her on to the corral, turned her in, and went to our camp behind the barn.

As near as I could judge, it was about ten o'clock, so I expected to find the other fellows sleeping, but they weren't. When I came around the corner of the barn they were all fully dressed and standing in a knot by the pup tent. Doc stepped toward me and whispered, "Hudson's on a tear. Must have missed the pony when he drove in."

"Did he come back here?" I asked.

"No," he said. "Went right to the house, but he was bawling like a bull after he got in there. Couldn't make out what it was all about, but he was sure madder'n a bear in a trap."

The other fellows had gathered around us, looking worried, so I told them, "Then there's nothing to worry about. If he didn't dare come back here when he first found the mare missing he won't dare come now. Sit down and let me tell you about the deal I made in town."

Paco was as curious as any of the others, and probably a bit more worried for fear there was trouble brewing. Before I started my story I gave him the blanket roll, told him in Spanish that everything was going to be all right, and asked if he'd like to make beds for Doc and me while I talked to the others. I didn't hold anything back in telling them the story, but tried to keep the language simple enough that Gus, Lars, and Jaikus could understand it clearly.

Before I'd finished Gus and Lars were looking at each other and nodding their heads, but I didn't want to let anyone speak until I'd told my whole plan, so I said, "This is the way I've figured it out: Today we kept three barges on the run because Hudson was taking a lot more straw than necessary, and because you had to chase him around that forty-acre field. Two barges could have done it without any running if he'd taken only enough straw to get all the heads, and if the stacks had been at the center of the field instead of at one end. Then if he hadn't tried to run his horses and had the breakdowns, we could have harvested the forty acres in ten hours instead of fourteen. If we go at it the right way, I think eight of us can harvest fifty acres in a thirteen-hour day. At two dollars an acre, that's a hundred bucks. I'll take out twenty for horses, equipment, and grub, then if we split the balance between us it will give us ten dollars apiece. If we can't finish by the end of the month, and I have to settle for a dollar and a half an acre, you'll still draw ten dollars apiece for every fifty acres we've harvested, and I'll take the other five to cover the grub. Is that a fair deal?"

Every one of them said it was, that they'd stick by me, and would gamble on any wages they earned before the attachments were served. "Then this is what we'd better do," I told them. "We won't be working tomorrow, or Hudson wouldn't have had the horses turned out to pasture. As soon as we've had breakfast we'll clear out of here, and stay away till bed time. In that way we'll keep out of any wrangles with him, and we'll be here for breakfast Monday morning. Let's turn in and get what sleep we can; it must be nearly midnight."

I'd forgotten about Paco during our talk, but when Doc and I went to the beds he'd made for us he was sitting in the middle of his own; knees drawn up, sombrero on, and his colorful blanket wrapped around his shoulders. I'd have spoken to him and told him to get some sleep, except that Doc was wound up like a dollar watch. "Tell you what we'll do, Bud," he was saying. "I always swore I'd never get another callous on my hands, but as soon as this deal goes through I'll take on the stacking job, and you run the header. We ought to clean up a couple of hundred bucks apiece by the end of the month, then you and I'll go into the medicine-show business—and brother, we'll clean up a fortune."

"We'll talk about it when this job is over," I told him, "but let's get some sleep now; I'm tuckered."

I'd crawled into my folded blanket before I noticed that Paco was still sitting up with his around his shoulders. I whispered for him to lie down and get some sleep, but he mumbled that he wasn't sleepy yet.

6

Completamente Aplastada

SOMETIMES I have trouble in going to sleep when I'm a bit worried, but the night I made the deal with Bones I must have blanked out the moment Paco answered me. The next thing I knew, Hudson bellowed, "All hands out!"

My eyes snapped open just in time to see Paco leap to his feet, his blanket flying in mid-air, and a pitchfork clutched in his hands, but Hudson was nowhere in sight. Paco said he'd never come as far as the corner of the barn, but shouted before he got there, and turned back. There was no doubt that he planned to work that day, for it couldn't have been later than quarter-past-four. "Well?" Doc asked, as much as to say, "Are we going to work or not?"

"Let's go do it," I told the fellows, "but stay away from Hudson, and don't blow up if he yells at you. If he wants to start trouble, let him start it with me; I'm the one he's mad at."

A lamp was lit in the kitchen, and as we went to the windmill to wash we could see Hudson eating at the table. He came out and headed for the barn just as we finished washing. Breakfast was on the table, the door to the next room stood slightly ajar, and the house was deathly still. We filed in, took our places, and had begun eating in silence when I heard the jumble of a panicked horse's hoofs in the yard. It was followed by Hudson's voice, swearing and angry, and by a rhythmic cracking of the blacksnake. We all sat with our mouths full, but not chewing, as the sounds went on for a full two minutes or more. A moment later Hudson streaked past the windmill on Kitten, and I caught a glimpse of him through the window, spurring viciously, and beating her with the doubled black-snake. After a few minutes, Doc mumbled, "Let's get out of here."

I was the last in line, and was just leaving the kitchen when Judy called in a frightened voice, "Bud." As I turned she came running across the kitchen to me, clutched my shirt sleeves hysterically, and told me, "Bud, you got to get away from here! You got to get away quick! Myron will kill you. He says he's going to learn you and Kitten a lesson you'll neither of you never forget, and he's learnt Kitten hers a'ready. If you're here when he brings the horses in he'll get you sure."

Judy had on her working clothes, with the cap pulled so far down that I couldn't see her face, so I put my hand under her chin and turned it up to me. "No, he won't, Judy," I told her. "You just stop and think a minute. In the first place, he wouldn't dare to touch me with the crew around; he knows Paco would kill him. In the second place, he doesn't dare touch me anyway. He didn't know the others were awake when I rode in last night. If he wanted to catch me alone, he'd have laid for me when I was putting Kitten into the corral. He'll do a lot of yelling, and trying to egg me into starting something, but that's as far as he'll go."

She still clung to me, and her lips trembled as she said, "You don't know him, Bud. He's a'ready beat up . . ."

"I know all about it," I broke in. "Bones told me last night. Things are going to be all right, and I'm going to stay right here, maybe till the end of the month. I won't let him start any trouble—not if he cusses me till sundown. Now you run along and get some breakfast; the boys are waiting for me." As

I said it, I leaned over, kissed her on the forehead, and went out.

The other fellows were standing in a knot by the corral gate, Jaikus jabbering to Old Bill, Gus and Lars looking stolid, and Paco leaning on a pitchfork. When I was halfway across the yard, Doc called to me, "Let's get away from here. Crazy or not, this man isn't safe to be around."

I didn't answer him till I reached the gate, then said, "It's up to you fellows. I can't tell you what to do; I can only tell you what I'm going to do. I'm going to stay right here. If we leave now we'll brand ourselves as yellow; if we stay, Hudson will brand himself that color."

Then, to give them a little chance to think, I turned to Paco, told him there'd be no need of the pitchfork, and asked if he'd like to milk the cows for the señora. When I turned back, Gus and Lars were nodding to each other, and Jaikus was nudging Old Bill. It was enough to let me know that I'd turned the crew my way for the moment, but I couldn't be sure it would stay turned if we just stood waiting for Hudson to bring the horses in, so I said, "Those barge wheels have dried out enough that they'll fall to pieces before the day's over unless we get 'em off and put to soak."

It probably took us a half hour to take the wheels off and put them to soak in the tank, but there was no sign of Hudson, so I had a mental picture of him; chasing the frightened horse herd around the pasture, cursing, lashing, and trying to drive them into the lane. Paco had finished milking and was carrying the buckets to the house when he suddenly set them down and came running to me, shouting, "*El jefe! El jefe! Completamente aplastada!*"

My Spanish was far from good, but I knew that *jefe* meant *boss,* and that *aplastada* meant *crushed* or *smashed.* For a moment I couldn't make sense out of what Paco was shouting, then he turned and pointed toward the windmill. Beyond it, and part way down the pasture lane, Kitten came slowly, turned quartering, and dragging a motionless load from the off stirrup of the saddle. None of us needed to be told what she was dragging, and we all ran toward her, but at sight of us she spooked and turned back toward the pasture. I motioned the others to wait, then walked ahead slowly, keeping up a steady babble of talk, just loud enough to reach Kitten's ears.

At the sound of my voice she stopped, swung her head toward me, and stood with it high, ears erect, ready to plunge away if I made a quick move. I stood and waited a minute or more for her nerves to let down a bit, then moved on again, talking all the while. She kept her head high and her ears up until she caught my scent, then all the sap seemed to drain out of her. Her head drooped, and she stood quietly while I went to her. I had to pass Hudson's body to reach her. One foot was hung in the stirrup, with the end of the whip coiled twice around it, binding it as tightly as a living blacksnake could have.

There was no reason to hurry about releasing the foot, but Kitten needed comforting if ever a horse did. She was trembling in every nerve and muscle, and I had to pet and stroke her several minutes before the trembling quieted. Then I untied the latigo straps, let the cinch fall free, and eased the saddle to the ground. It wasn't until then that I looked back toward the house. The others, with Judy and her sister among them, were standing by the windmill, motionless, and looking toward us as sheep will stare at a sight that awes them.

I led Kitten to the mill, passed the reins to Paco, and told him to put her in the corral. Then I went straight to Mrs. Hudson. She was dry eyed, and I could see no grief in her face; only horror and confusion. "There's nothing that can be done," I told her. "If a bed can be made ready, we'll bring him to the house."

She just stood, looking at me in a confused sort of way for maybe a minute, then asked, "Could you wait till Judy takes the children away? She can drive the. . . ." Before she could finish the sentence she slumped in a dead faint, but Doc caught her, lifted her in his arms, and carried her to the house.

Judy had seemed awestruck until her sister fainted, then she became nearly hysterical. She started to follow Doc, then turned and ran back to me, clutched my sleeves convulsively, and pleaded, "Don't bring him, Bud! Don't bring him now! Don't let the children see him! With Sis fainted and all, I don't know when I can take 'em away. Bud, you won't. . . ."

With each word she was becoming more hysterical, so I put an arm around her, led her toward the house, and told her, "Of course I won't, Judy, and with a doctor right here to take care of your sister there's no reason for you to worry about her. We'll cover Myron with a blanket and stay away from here till after you've gone. In that way the children will never know anything has happened. Where are you going to take them?"

"Home," she told me. "Paw and my other sister will look after 'em. I'll be back in not more'n an hour."

"Before you come," I told her, "stop and tell Bones what has happened. He'll need to know before he makes some phone calls that he was planning to make. And you tell your sister that I'll stay right here until her crop is harvested."

Judy hadn't looked up at me as we walked from the windmill to the kitchen doorway, but as I took my arm away and she stepped inside, she looked up with her eyes brimming and said, "God bless you, Bud. I'll never forget you as long as I live." As if she were ashamed of what she'd said, she ran across the kitchen to the door that still stood ajar at the far side.

I motioned to the other fellows and started slowly toward the barn. When they caught up with me I told them, "The best thing we can do is to stay out of sight till the children are taken away. I'll carry a blanket up and cover the body, but we'll leave it where it is till they're gone."

I'd little more than glanced at Hudson when I went to get Kitten, but when I took the blanket back I could see that Paco had chosen the right words when he'd said, *Completamente aplastada.* The chest was crushed almost flat. There was blood around the mouth and nose, and at both sides of the shirt, where broken ribs had cut through the skin. But even though the sun was less than an hour high, the bloodstains were dry. There could be only one answer: when Kitten had taken all the punishment she could stand she'd caught him with the whip wound around his foot, and had thrown herself over backwards before he could jump clear. It could only be that she'd done it almost immediately after he'd ridden her into the pasture, and that it had taken her the rest of the time to drag his body back. I didn't stop to release the foot from the stirrup, but spread the blanket over saddle and all, then turned back to our camp behind the barn.

There is seldom any reason to grieve for the dead; only for those who are left behind. And in Hudson's case there was no reason to grieve for them. I was the only one who could be in any way injured by his death. With him gone, there was no reason for any banker to foreclose a mortgage or put an attachment on the crop, and without them my deal would certainly be as dead as Hudson.

At our camp I told the other fellows what I thought had happened, and that our deal would be off, then we sat in silence until we heard the old Maxwell backfire as Judy started it and drove away. When I went to the house, I found Doc helping Mrs. Hudson clear one of the front rooms and make up a bed in it. The room was almost barren, its only furniture a packing box with flour sacks tacked around it to make a table, and an old iron bed that sagged deeply in the middle. Doc was at one side and Mrs. Hudson at the other, drawing a patched sheet up over the stained mattress. She looked up as I stepped into the doorway, and said, "You could bring Myron in now; Judy has took the children to my folks." There was neither grief nor emotion in her voice or face; only a sort of blank confusedness.

No matter how much a man may have been despised, his remains demand some reverence, so we made a stretcher from two boards, laid the body on it, straightened the legs, folded the hands, and wrapped the blanket from my bed around the whole litter. Then Gus and Lars carried it to the house. Mrs.

Hudson stood emotionless while they laid the blanket-shrouded litter on the bed, then Doc put a hand under her elbow and led her to the kitchen, while the rest of us went to our camp. There was nothing to say or do, so I did what I'd always done when there was time to be waited out; found a piece of wood, whetted my jackknife on the sole of my boot, and began whittling a little horse. I'd done it ever since I was old enough to carry a knife, and nothing ever made time slip away faster.

I'd whittled only enough to outline the head and neck when I heard an automobile drive into the yard and stop. I knew it couldn't be Judy, because there was no clattering, and the engine ran smoothly until it was shut off. With Doc at the house there was no reason for my going, so I kept on with my whittling for maybe another half hour. Then I heard Judy drive in, and a few minutes later she came to the corner of the barn and called, "Bud, Sis and Bones want to talk to you." She didn't wait for me, and was out of sight by the time I'd put my whittling away and gone around the barn.

When I reached the corner of the house Doc and Judy were sitting on the windmill platform, talking, and when I went to the back door Mrs. Hudson and the banker were seated at the kitchen table. "Come in, Son," Bones said when he looked up and saw me, "there's some things we'd better talk about. Sit here where we can look at each other."

"I understand," I said, and took a chair opposite him.

For maybe a minute after I'd taken the seat, Bones looked down at his hands, pulling one finger after another until the knuckles snapped. It was plain enough that he didn't like to tell me what he was going to, and I knew well enough what it would be. After he'd cracked all five knuckles, he looked up and said, "Last night I made you an out-and-out promise that I'd foreclose on Myron's horses, equipment and harness, and let you have the whole works on a note for three hundred dollars."

Then he stopped and cracked another knuckle, so I said, "That's right, but you didn't know what was going to happen then, any more than I did. There'd be no sense in foreclosing now, and I'll never try to hold you to the deal." As I said it I took the memorandum out of my pocket and pushed it across the table toward him.

That time he cracked two knuckles before he said, "We shook hands on it, didn't we, Son?"

"Sure," I said, "and I'll shake with you again to release you."

"*That's* what I wanted to hear," he said, "and what I wanted Clara to hear. I wanted her to know what kind of a man she was dealing with. We've talked the whole thing over, and she wants to go through with the deal just the way we made it last night. She won't have any use for horses after this crop is in, and if it's as good as I think, she'll be well fixed for years to come. Of course you understand there won't be any attachments now, and your deal will be with Clara, not me or the other lien holders, but she's told me to open that account for you, just like we talked about, and to credit it every week with what you've harvested. Do you want that I make out a new paper for her to sign?"

"There's no need of it as far as I'm concerned," I told him. "I'd trust her as far as I would my own sister, but if she'd rather have a written agreement I'd be glad to sign it."

Mrs. Hudson had been sitting as though she had no part in the deal, looking down in an unseeing manner at her folded hands. When I'd finished speaking she raised her head, looked squarely into my eyes, and said, "I'm beholden to you for what you've a'ready done around the place . . . giving me a hand with the milking . . . putting the barges into shape . . . and promising to stay on through harvest and thrashing. There's no man I'd leaver have take care of the crop . . . or to have the horses . . . half of 'em are colts of my little mare, Vixen . . . she passed on last winter. I don't want no paper less'n you do."

"Then I reckon we've got a deal," the banker broke in. As he spoke he reached in his pocket, bringing out a checkbook and a signature card. He pushed them across the table toward me, and said, "Better put your John Hancock on that card, so we'll know your checks when they come in. Clara's going to stay a few days with her folks . . . till the funeral's over . . . but Judy'll come out and do the cooking for you—you'll look after her, won't you, Son?—and if you'll give her a list of the grub you want she'll fetch it out this morning . . . Joe'll open up to get it for her. Think you can make out all right?"

"I wouldn't be much of a man if I couldn't make out with backing like this," I told him, "and I want you to know that I thank you for your confidence—both of you."

"Don't thank me," Bones chuckled; "thank Judy. I couldn't get the little tyke off my coat tail till I'd promised to come right on out here and get things buttoned up for you to boss the job. Clara thought, like I did, that the best thing to do was to go on through with the deal you and I made in the first place. She's going to ride back to town with me after the undertaker comes—I've phoned him so he'll be along pretty soon. When there's anything I can do for you, let me know; I'll be dropping out now and again to see how you're getting on."

There was little more left to say, so I thanked Mrs. Hudson again, and asked, "Did Mr. Hudson get the new conveyor belts for the header last night?"

"No, he didn't," she told me, "and that's partly what he was so mad about. They wouldn't leave him have 'em without he paid cash."

"Could I get them at The Bluffs?" I asked Bones. "I'm afraid the ones we've got now are too rotten to run another day."

"No, not for an old fifteen-foot header like this one—there can't be more than three or four of 'em left in the country," he told me. "You'd have to go to Oberlin to get 'em, but the Co-operative keeps open on Sundays in harvest time, and they'll take your check all right. Get anything you need, and I'll phone 'em and tell 'em you're good for it. If you talked real sweet to Judy I reckon she'd drive you over there. You could come by The Bluffs and pick up your grub on the way back. Joe'll be up and about by that time, and it would save you making up a list."

7

On My Own

WHEN I left the kitchen after my talk with Bones and Mrs. Hudson, Doc and Judy were still sitting on the windmill platform. I went right to them and asked, "Doc, would you ask the others to come up here? We've got a little business to talk about."

Judy was as eager and jumpy as a race horse at the barrier when I sat down beside her. Doc was barely out of earshot before she took hold of my sleeve, twiddled it nervously, and asked, "You're going to boss the harvesting, ain't you, Bud? Sis said she wanted you to, and I talked to Bones, and he said . . ."

I took her hand off my sleeve, but didn't let go of it, and broke in, "Yes, Judy girl, and more than that; I'm going to be in business for myself on it. We've made a deal that I'll hire the crew, feed it, and harvest the whole crop. If I get it done by the end of the month, all the horses and equipment will be mine, and I'll have made a good stake to boot. It's going to be a big job—bigger than I can handle unless the fellows stand close behind me and want to see me win out. Can I count on you to help me with it?"

She looked up into my face earnestly, and told me, "You know I'll help you all 1 can, Bud. Till Sis comes back I'll have to sleep to home, but I'll come early in the mornings, and stay till everything is took care of at nights, and I can pitch wheat almost as good as any man my size. I could . . ."

"Yes, you could kill yourself in about three days if I'd let you, but I'm not going to," I said. "We'll get our own breakfasts, and take care of the milk and dishes after supper, but you can do the rest of the cooking and dishes, then drive barge for Gus and Lars in what extra time you have—that is, if the rest of the crew sees this the way I do. That'll give you both hands full, because I plan to be a harder slave driver than Myron was."

Judy sat looking down at our hands for a minute, rubbing her thumb along mine. Then without looking up, she asked, "What you going to do when the harvest's ended, Bud?"

"I don't know," I told her, "but I like that valley where the bluffs are; it looks to me like awfully good cattle country. If I win out on this job and get the horses, and a little stake, I might stay around a while and try to get a small place of my own—not farming, but cattle. 1 worked with them when I was a little kid, and I guess I got cattle and horses into my blood. I've always told myself I'd be a cattleman when I grew up, and I'm just about there. I'll be twenty-one in December. If I'm ever going into the business it's about time I made a start."

We let go of each other's hand when we heard the shuffle of boots, and were talking about going to Oberlin for conveyer belts when Doc came back with the crew. "Sit down and let's do a little chinning," I told them. "An hour ago I thought the deal I told you about last night was all off, but it isn't. The bankers are out of it now, but Mrs. Hudson has made me the same proposition, and I've taken it. Last night I was figuring on hiring another man to make up a crew of eight, but Judy thinks she could cook for us and help in the field too. If she does, we might get along without another man, but she'd share with the rest of us on the money. Gus and Lars would have to get along without a driver for a couple of hours a day, and somebody would have to pitch in on cooking breakfast and washing the supper dishes. It's up to you fellows: what'll we do; get another man, or say we've got one?"

Judy was still in her rolled-up overalls and jumper, and with her cap pulled down over her hair she looked—from the back —more like a boy than a girl. She kept her head down while I was talking, but when I asked the question she peeked nervously along the line of faces. There was no question about the decision: Gus and Lars began nodding at each other, and Doc volunteered to help with the cooking and dishwashing. Even though Paco couldn't understand a word, he seemed to know what was going on, and his smile showed that he was all for the idea.

"All right," I said, "now that we know who's on the team we'd better get lined out on what we're going to do next. Judy's going to drive me to town for new conveyor belts and a load of groceries. Before we start, Doc, let's go over the old header, so I can pick up whatever other parts need to be replaced, and tools for doing the job. Paco can mend harness and make check straps to replace those jockey poles, and the rest of you might see what you can do about making two decent barges out of those three old wrecks. Let's get everything shipshape today, so we'll be ready to tackle the job bright and early in the morning."

By the time I'd told Paco I was going to be his new boss, and what I wanted him to do, Doc was at the header and the other four were fishing barge wheels out of the tank. Within half an hour I had a list of the new parts and tools we'd need, and Judy was waiting for me by the old Maxwell. She'd changed into her bright gingham dress, and looked as pert as a robin in the spring. She jiggled the choke wire while I turned the crank, and the old jalopy backfired as if she thought it was still the Fourth of July and she had all the firecrackers. She was still backfiring when Judy clashed her into gear, and we went streaking out of the yard. Considering the roads, Judy was a fast driver, and she talked nearly as fast as she drove. If I hadn't already been pretty well sold on Beaver Valley as a good place to go into the cattle business, she'd have sold me long before we reached Oberlin.

Bones must have phoned the man at the Co-operative before we got there, for he was certainly co-operative. He seemed more than anxious to please me, got me everything I asked for, and reminded me of some I'd forgotten. When I fished out my checkbook he could have seen that it was brand new, but I didn't want him to know I was writing the first check I'd ever written in my life, so I numbered it 101. And before I filled in the amount I looked up and said, "It being Sunday, I'm a little short of cash; mind if I make it out for an extra five?"

"Not a bit," he told me. "Make it out for whatever you want; I've got plenty of cash on hand today."

I didn't want Judy to know that I didn't have a solitary nickel, but I did want to buy her an ice-cream soda while we were in a town big enough that we could get one. She seemed willing enough to have me do it, and I've bought ice-cream sodas for a lot of girls I didn't like as well.

Driving around to Cedar Bluffs on our way back to the place took us about ten miles out of our way, but we were busy enough talking that the trip didn't seem very far. As soon as we'd pulled out of Oberlin I told Judy, "I want to set the best table any-where around. You do the ordering, and buy enough stuff to run us all the way through harvest. One of the first things my father taught me about ranching was that the boss who sets the best table, and who feeds his horses best, is the one who has the least trouble and gets the most done."

Judy pulled the old Maxwell over to the side of the road, fished a stubby pencil out of her handbag, and told me to write things down as she called them off to me, so we'd know just what we wanted when we reached Joe's store. Before we reached it I thought she must be planning to set up a grocery store of our own.

"Of course," she said, "we can't buy enough fresh meat or eggs to go all the way through, 'cause they'd go bad on us. You can't keep much of that kind of things without you've got ice or a dug well to let 'em down into. Up on the divide they're all drilled wells, so there's no place to keep nothing cool. But we'll get a hind quarter of pork—off'n a good young barrow—so there'll be fresh ham for breakfasts, and pork chops for suppers, and plenty of side meat for dinners. And I don't reckon we'd best to get more'n ten dozen eggs to start off with, and let's see . . . a sack of white flour—soft wheat, for biscuits—and a sack of spuds, and a sack of beans . . . do you like the pinto kind?"

"I like them to beat the band," I told her, "but I can't eat them if I stay on my diet. The reason I'm so skinny is that I have diabetes, so I'm supposed to eat only green vegetables and a kind of bread I won't be able to get here, along with chicken, eggs, nuts, fish, and things like that."

"Well, there's bullheads in the creek," she said, "but we won't have no time to go fishing, leastways not till harvest's over."

"Canned salmon is all right," I said, "and I'm used to it. I've lived on it and eggs and cabbage for the past eight months."

"Cabbage?" she said, and jumped her foot off the gas pedal. "Why didn't you tell me when we was in Oberlin? Joe, he don't carry fresh stuff like that. Would sauerkraut do?"

"Sure," I told her.

"Well, put down a case of it. Joe keeps peanuts—a whole barrel of 'em—and we got plenty of chickens to home. I'll bring out some tomorrow. Myron wouldn't have none on the place; said one hen would ruin more crops than a herd of cattle. Peas and beans—green ones—ought to be all right for vegetables. Put down a case of each one, and a case of hominy, and pears, and peaches, and apple sauce—it goes awful good with pork chops. Did I tell you onions? They're mighty good in fried spuds for breakfast . . . and baking powder, and syrup . . . I can make good flapjacks."

When we reached The Bluffs, Joe was sitting in front of his store, his chair tilted back in the shade under the canopy. Of course he'd known Judy all her life, and he recognized me as soon as we pulled up beside the hitch rail. Without tilting his chair down, he called, "Oh, so you're the one! Reckoned there was somethin' in the wind when Bones give you that note last night. He tells me Myron was kilt by that feisty little old mare of his. How'd she do it, tromp him?"

As we climbed out of the jalopy I told him, "I wasn't there when it happened, so I couldn't tell you. Would you like to get us out a load of groceries? I'll give you a check for them."

Joe brought his chair down with a thump, jumped to his feet, and fumbled around as he fitted a key into the door lock. With his back to us he called heartily, "Come right on in and pick out what you want. No need to pay for it now; you can leave it go till the month end. Bones, he'll stand good for it if you don't."

Joe was in such a hurry that he was inside the store before Judy and I had reached the shade of the canopy. "The old boy must be kind of hungry for business," I whispered to her.

"You can't blame him," she whispered back. "Any more, folks go to the Co-op over to Oberlin for their big orders—them that can pay cash. About all Joe gets is the fill-ins, and the charge-it-till-harvest-time business."

I don't know which one of us had the most fun; Joe in gloating over the business he was getting, Judy in doing her shopping, or I in watching them both. She bustled around the store as if she'd been the banker's wife, and she was a sharp little trader. Whether or not she actually knew the prices at the Co-operative, she made Joe think she did. She took a can of peas down from the shelf and called, "How much you asking for these Arbuckle peas, Joe?"

"Fourteen cents," he called back.

"You're too dear on 'em," she told him. "Over to the Co-op they're twelve—six for seventy cents."

"I could leave you have them M-H brand—right there to your left—for eleven," he shouted back from the counter.

"Don't want 'em," she sang out. "We don't aim to go hunting no jack rabbits, and them M-H's are harder'n buckshot. How much a case for these Arbuckles?"

After a minute's thought Joe shouted, "Bein' it's a big order, I'd leave you have 'em for three dollars."

Judy mumbled to herself, "Six into twenty-four is four, times seventy," then called back, "I'll give you two-seventy-five; that's what they'd cost over to the Co-op."

On each item Joe met her price, and as I carried the cases out to the Maxwell I went past the counter to see that he wrote them down correctly on the bill.

It was nearly noon when we got back to the ranch, and the old Maxwell was loaded to the top rail. Doc was busy at the header, Paco was repairing harness, and the others were working on the barges. Judy turned sharply at the corner of the milking pen and drove to the back door of the house. While she gathered up a few of the smaller packages, I took the new conveyor belts and what I could carry of the spare parts and supplies, then went to see how Doc was getting along. He was on his knees, and had worn parts scattered all around him. As I came toward him he climbed to his feet and told me, "The undertaker came right after you left, and the banker took the Missis away as soon as the hearse had gone. I'd be further along with this job only we had a funeral of our own; buried what was left of that boar pork deep enough the dogs couldn't dig it up. From the looks of that load you brought in, I guess we'll manage to get by without it."

"If you're going to be the kitchen canary you might as well get started on the job by lugging the stuff in and helping Judy get some dinner ready," I told him. "I don't know about the rest of you, but right now I'm hungry enough to put away half of what we brought. How are they making out with the barges? Think we can get them patched up enough to last out the harvest?"

"Say, those Swedes are all right!" Doc told me. "Bet you a hat they're carpenters by trade. Go take a look at what they're doing with those wheels, and I'll go wrastle up some grub."

When I reached the barges I was sure Doc had been right in his guess. Gus and Lars had taken all twelve of the rickety old wheels apart, had sorted out the best spokes, hubs, and fellies, and had already reassembled four good solid wheels. I stopped just long enough to tell them what a fine job they were doing, then went on to Old Bill and Jaikus. Neither of them was worth a nickel as a carpenter, but they were doing the best they could, so I passed them the sacks of nails I'd brought, and told them they were doing okay, and then went on to Paco. He was doing more than okay.

Except for two sets, the harness was nothing but a collection of neglected junk, but Paco had the two worst sets put into fairly good condition. In all his life he'd probably never known anything but patched-up harness, and had learned to do more tricks with wire, a pair of pliers, and a couple of rocks than any man I'd ever known. He was as excited as a little youngster with the sack of new snaps, buckles, and rivets I'd brought from town. I stayed with him, telling him about the deal I'd made, until Doc called, "Come and get it 'fore I throw it to the coyotes!"

I hadn't heard that old chuckwagon call since I'd been a kid in Colorado. At any other time I'd have been glad to hear it, but it seemed out of place on a day when a man had been killed. My feeling must have been evident in my voice when I called back, "We'll be along in a few minutes." Usually men will start on the run when the chuckwagon call is given, but no one left his work until I led the way to the wash basin at the windmill.

As always, we waited to go in together. When we reached the kitchen we found Doc and Judy as proud as peacocks, and they had reason to be. The table was spread with flour sacks for a cloth, and enough food for two dozen hungry men. There was a big platter of fresh ham steaks, another of hashed-brown potatoes, two heaping plates of biscuits, and they'd opened at least two cans of every sort of vegetable and fruit we'd bought. There weren't bowls enough to hold all the stuff, so they'd just opened the cans of fruit and set them on as they were. The only single can they'd opened was salmon. It was standing beside a

steaming hot bowl of sauerkraut, at the end of the table where
Hudson had always sat.

For some reason I didn't want to sit at that place, but there
was nothing else to do, so I went around and stopped behind
the chair. The table was set with three plates on each side and
one on each end. Doc drew back the chair at the end opposite
me, and bowed low toward Judy. Her face turned scarlet, and
for a few seconds she looked confused, then she stepped forward and let Doc seat her.

No one helped himself until the platter, bowl, or coffee pot
had been passed to Judy and came back to him around the
table, and no one could seem to think of anything to say. To
break the tension, I told Doc I'd like him to take a walk through
both sections with me, so we could find which quarters were
most apt to shatter and should be harvested first. I didn't
know enough about wheat to trust my own judgment, but
from what Doc had told me about stacking I was sure that he
knew, and that we could save Mrs. Hudson a lot of wheat by
harvesting the ripest and driest first. From there on, everyone
seemed at ease, and the conversation was all about the job we
had ahead of us.

It was one o'clock before we left the table, then it took Doc
and me about three hours to put the new parts on the header,
and to rig a heavy enough counterweight on the boom that I
could raise and lower the cutting head easily. After we'd finished, Judy drove us around both sections of uncut wheat. At
every quarter mile we drove a tall stake, and tied a white rag
to it, so we'd have markers for dividing the sections into forty-
acre fields. As we went along we walked deep enough into
each field to find out exactly the condition of the crop, and I
drew a map to show which quarters should be harvested first.
Where the land was level the kernels were already hardened,
but there was still enough sap in the straw to avoid any danger
of shattering for two or three weeks. On the highest rises the
grain was so dry it would begin shattering within a few days,
but where there were dips it could safely be left standing for

nearly a month.

In the deepest draw the grain stood waist-high, the kernels were still in the milk stage, and the leaves were green. "This would make pretty good horse feed," Doc told me. "Cut now, it would give 'em both hay and grain, but these heads are too heavy for the limber stalks. Leave it till it's ripe, with these hot winds blowing, and most of it would go down too flat to be harvested."

"Then let's come and get a load of it," I told him. "It will give me a chance to try the header out—and the horses too. I'm afraid they may have gone wilder than chicken hawks again after a day in the pasture."

It was probably five o'clock before we got back from checking the fields, so I started the men right off to the pasture, telling them where to take positions, and to make no move that might frighten the horses. As soon as they'd gone I went to the corral for Kitten. Her sides were still streaked with dried blood from the spurring she'd had, but she seemed to be well over her fright and nervousness. There was no hurry, for it would take the crew ten or fifteen minutes to get into position, so I worked slowly with Kitten—talking to her from outside the corral before I went in. I wasn't yet ready to try her with a saddle; first because I thought she might associate it with Hudson, and secondly because his stirrups would be three or four inches too long for me. I expected that she'd do as she had always done; make a run for the far end of the corral, but she didn't. She stood without even laying back her ears, and let me walk straight to her. I slipped the bridle on, stroked her neck a minute or two, led her out through the gate, propped it wide open, and flipped onto her back.

After I'd watered Kitten I closed the gate at the end of the lane, and flipped onto her back again. That time she acted nervous, raised her head high, and pointed her ears sharply up the lane. I let her take her time, moving forward a few steps, stopping to sniff the air, then moving on again. When we reached the place where I'd come to relieve her of her burden that morning, she approached it dancing and trembling, shied away from the spot where the body had lain, then raced past as though a ghost had risen behind her. I'd managed to quiet her a little, but she was still trembling when I rode her into the pasture. A hundred yards or so farther on she shied again, and circled wide around a spot where the ground was trampled.

The horse herd was at the same place Hudson and I had found it, and again raced away into the gulch as I rode into the pasture. I let Kitten lope to the north, then took her down into the bottleneck of the gulch, just as we had gone before, and again I found the herd trotting toward me on the wide grassy floor. At sight of it Kitten wanted to charge, but I held her to a jogging trot. For maybe a minute, the herd stopped and stood watching us, heads high, and ready to spook at our first quick move. When we didn't make one, the horses trotted back the way they had come, and, with the men strung out to head them off, we had no trouble in turning them into the lane.

We waited at the end of the lane until the horses had time to reach the gate at the far end and quiet down, then cut the colts back to the pasture, let the others stop to drink at the tank, and drove them on quietly to the corral. By working slowly with them, they didn't give us much trouble harnessing.

There was no need of using more than one barge for hauling feed, so we harnessed only eight horses, taking the three teams that had worked on the barges the previous day, along with the two heaviest colts from the header teams. I had Old Bill hitch the colts to the barge, and we put the better-broken six on the header, for I knew I'd have trouble enough in handling it for the first time, even though I had horses that wouldn't require too much driving. Then, before we started out, I made a few turns in the yard, so as to give the horses, as well as myself, a little practice at turning corners.

With the machine out of gear, and there in the yard where the ground was smooth and hard, I didn't have to fight the rudder, and the horses soon got the idea of swinging off to the side in making the turns. By the time we'd made six or eight of them I could come fairly close to putting the old header right on the lines I had Doc mark for me. "That's enough," I told him. "Suppose you give Judy a hand with supper while we're gone. We'll be back in less than an hour."

The draw we were going to take the feed from was nearly a mile from the house, so I got in some more good practice on the way, and it was lucky that I did. It took us till sundown to harvest that one load of horse feed. I'd learned a good deal about handling a header before the barge was loaded, but that little draw looked about the way my brother's head did the first time I practiced haircutting on him. Even so, I'd been fortunate enough that, with all my blunders and mishaps, no part of the machine had been broken.

Doc and I had picked a forty-acre field farther from the house for our first day's harvesting, so there was no sense in taking the header back to the yard. We unhitched the horses, slipped the bits out of their mouths, and tied them to the back of the barge, so they could help themselves on the way home. Then, while Paco and I unharnessed, Bill and Jaikus pitched the load tight against the corral fence, so the horses could eat as much as they wanted during the night.

That afternoon Gus and Lars had not only repaired the remaining wheels for two barges, but had built Judy a cooler box outside the kitchen window. When covered with wet straw, the evaporation would cool it enough to keep meat, butter, and eggs fresh for a week or so.

Supper had been ready for an hour before we'd finished our chores, but Judy had kept it hot on the back of the stove, and it was as good a meal as dinner had been. During the afternoon she'd scrubbed the kitchen until the floor boards gleamed, and she seemed to like sitting at the end of the table opposite me. The more the crew ate the happier she seemed, and they gave her plenty to be happy about. At that one meal they must have stowed away ten pounds of pork chops, and I cleaned up a whole can of salmon.

Paco had done the milking and separating before we got back with the horse feed, and after supper we all pitched in on the dishwashing. I was drying the last cup when Judy asked, "What time do you aim to get into the field in the morning, Bud? I'll come in plenty of time to cook breakfast while you're harnessing."

"It's up to you fellows," I told the crew, "but this is what's been going through my head: The more acreage we can put into the stacks in a day the more money we'll make, but if we go at it too hard we'll play the horses out, and the hotter it is the faster they'll give out. If we get into the field at sunup, lay off two hours for rest at noon, then work till sundown, it would give us a thirteen-hour day. That's enough to kill most horses, but if we do it the right way, I think thése tough little mustangs might stand up to it. If they don't, we'll just have to cut down to whatever time they can stand.

"It won't be rough on the barge horses, since they get a good rest during unloading. It's the header horses I'm worried about, and I think we can split the work up so that won't be too tough. With twelve horses and only two barges, we can lay each pair off every sixth day. Then if we trade around so the six that are on the header in the forenoon either lay off in the afternoon or are used on the barges, no horse will have a full day of killing work. In that way, and with a two-hour rest at noon, I think they might stand up to a thirteen-hour day. Do you think you fellows can?"

When I asked the question I looked at Doc, because, as stacker, he'd be the one who would have to be on the go the whole thirteen hours, and in one day's stacking I'd learned how tough it was.

"Let's give it a try," he told me, "but there's no sense in Judy getting out here before sunrise; I'll wrastle up some ham and eggs while the rest of you harness and do the milking. She can clean up the mess whenever she gets here. Fair enough, kiddo?"

He looked at Judy when he asked the question, but she shook

her head. "No, it ain't fair at all, and I won't do it," she told him. "If I'm going to get a full share of the pay, I'm going to put in a full share of the hours, but I'd best to get started for home before Paw comes out to see where I'm at. Did you know it's ha'-past-eight a'ready?"

8

Wheat Harvest

I can usually set my head so it works like an alarm clock, and before I turned in on the night of the accident I set it for four o'clock, but that wasn't a minute too early. The stars were still bright, and the sky had barely begun to turn gray in the east, when I heard the old Maxwell backfire as Judy drove into the yard. "Come help me, Bud," she called as I hauled on my jeans. "These ornery hens will scatter all over if we don't catch 'em."

Judy was herding three hens in the beam of the headlights, and three others craned their necks through holes in a sack that lay on the ground. "Come easy, and don't scare 'em till I turn the lights towards the barn door," she told me, "then we'll shoo 'em in there. The sack come untied when I took it out, and if they ever get into the wheat we'll never find 'em."

She backed the car around till the lights shone into the barn doorway, the hens went in by themselves, and with the other fellows helping me we had no trouble in catching them. When Doc passed one of them toward Judy, she said, "Dress it for me, will you? The boss, he can't eat no pork, so I want to put one on to stew for him while I'm cooking breakfast."

Even though Judy had called me the boss, I didn't have to do any bossing. Everyone seemed to know where he could be of the most help, and from there on we always did our chores exactly the same way every morning. Doc helped in the house, Gus and Lars did the milking, and Jaikus greased barge wheels and carried in corn cobs for the fire, while Paco, Bill, and I did the harnessing. The younger horses weren't too easy to handle, but didn't give us nearly as much trouble as on the first day, and we had all the teams ready for the field when Judy called, "Breakfast."

The edge of the sun was just peeping over the horizon when Paco and I hitched the horses to the header. I'd decided to use the same ones Hudson had used on Saturday, partly because they'd learned the trick of turning square corners, partly to wear the colts down a bit before putting them on the barges, and partly to give the old mares the first half-day's rest. To avoid any chance of the colts trying to run away with the header while it was out of gear and easy to pull, I had Bill drive his barge in front of us on the way to the new field, but there was no need of it. By my keeping a reasonably tight hand on the reins, the colts handled better than I expected, and we made a good square corner when we turned into the field.

Since we were to be paid by the acre, it seemed best to lay our work out in forty-acre tracts, each a quarter-mile square. Old Bill could drive a perfectly straight line, so I had him do all the driving on the first round of the forty we'd chosen for that day, using the markers Doc and I had put up as his guides. Then we cut our stackyard right at the center of the forty. I had a terrible time to control both the colts and machine, and to keep the wheat flowing into the barge on that first round, but any new job is a little rough until a fellow gets the knack of it.

With the laying out and cutting the stackyard, it was about an hour and a half after sunrise before we'd made our first round of the field. Then things went in pretty good shape. The colts had been fractious enough to keep my hands full during that first round, but as soon as they'd worked up a little sweat they steadied, though holding a little faster pace than I'd have liked. The first time around, I didn't have much chance to raise or lower the cutter, but once the horses settled down I kept watching ahead, and moving the boom often enough that we took only three or four inches of straw with the heads. By keeping the straw at a minimum, one barge could take the cut from a half-round of the field. And by starting in the middle, where we'd cut a roadway to the stackyard, we didn't waste a minute in chasing the header around the field.

Each time I reached the roadway, on either side of the field, there was an empty barge waiting for me, but each time I stopped to give my horses a few minutes' rest. At first, a half-round of the field loaded the barges almost to overflowing, no matter how careful I was in moving the boom so as to take only the minimum of straw. But as the morning went on and the field became smaller, the rounds went faster and the loads weren't so large.

The practice I'd had in cutting the horse feed had been tough enough to make my job out there in a fairly level field seem easy. But my muscles were still so soft that the continual pushing against the rudder with my legs, the constant raising and lowering of the boom, the handling of the reins, and their weight around my shoulders made me feel as though my whole body were one gigantic toothache. During the last hour before noon I might have rested the horses a few minutes longer than they needed, for they were still stepping right along, but I was so tired that my legs trembled. Of course, I realized that the field was becoming smaller with each round, but I was too busy to notice how much. It wasn't until we quit for noon that I took time to look it over, and I was surprised to find that we'd put nearly twenty-five acres into the stacks—and with only eight in the crew, instead of the eleven we'd had Saturday forenoon.

At about eleven o'clock I'd sent Judy in to get dinner ready. By the time we had the horses unharnessed, watered, and in the corral, she had everything on the table, and she'd laid herself out to give us as good a dinner as we'd had on Sunday. She had a whole stewed chicken in front of my plate, and I was so hungry that I ate nearly all of it. That dinner set a pattern for us without any planning. With our taking two hours off at noon, there was no reason to hurry, so we sat and talked for nearly half an hour after we'd finished eating—not about anything in particular, just talking and resting. Then, while Judy washed the dishes, we sat in the shade of the house and listened to Jaikus tell stories about the "ould sod" till it was time to harness.

In the afternoon we laid off the two youngest colts from the header teams, put the old mares in their places, then switched the other four to the barges, giving them an easier job for the rest of the day. I split the old mares, putting one on the outside of each header team, so as to balance the pull as much as I could. It balanced the pull all right, but they were slower walkers than the smaller, quicker-stepping mustangs. Still, it made my job easier, because I had to do no holding back on the reins, and the rudder required a lot less fighting. I made up for the lost time by shortening the rests when we changed barges, and well before the middle of the afternoon we'd finished our first forty acres.

With the lines of the first field to go by, it was no trick to lay out the second, though we lost a little time in cutting our center roadway and a stackyard. Even at that, I could see that we'd cut a good ten acres of the new forty when the sun was at least an hour high. I sent Judy in to get supper ready, and within a half hour the rest of us unhitched and called it a day. Both Doc and I had nearly reached the end of our ropes, but we had more than fifty acres of wheat in the stacks, and it made us both happy enough to forget how tired we were.

Supper went about as dinner had, we had a half-hour's visit at the table afterwards, then Gus and Lars went to do the milking while the rest of us helped Judy clear the table and wash the dishes. It had been about seven-thirty when the sun went down. By eight-thirty Judy was on her way back to town, and the rest of us were turning in between our blankets.

That first day set the pattern for our work. From then till
the end of harvest there was no bossing, and little planning,
for me to do. Each one in the crew not only did his—or her—
job well, but knew that if we were to finish by the end of July
we'd have to put fifty acres of wheat a day into the stacks, and
they wouldn't quit until another round or two had been added
for good measure. When we were in light, bone-dry grain it
was easy enough, then I'd call quits an hour before sundown.
After we'd skimmed off those first dry forties the going became
tougher, but we became tougher too. Within a few days Doc's
muscles and mine had hardened enough that the ache was
pretty well gone, and we'd picked up the knack of our jobs
enough that we didn't have to put so much strain on them.
Then too, the horses were working into as good shape as we
were. With plenty of feed and a lay-off of one day in six, they
came into lean, hard, excellent condition. And as soon as they
learned that there were no blacksnakes to fear, they gave no
trouble in either harnessing or handling.

The first break in our routine came on the Friday after we
started the job. In the middle of the forenoon a car turned into
the roadway toward the house. A few minutes later it went
back, and when Judy brought her empty barge to the header
she told me, "That was Paw's car; he's brought Sis and the
children home. There won't be no need for me to go in and
cook dinner; I've told her what we'll have, and Sis can cook
better'n me . . . when she's got anything to cook with. Paw
said he'd fetch out half a dozen more hens, so I put the last one
of the others on to stew this morning."

Judy went right to the house when we got in that noon, and
by the time we'd unharnessed and washed a cracking good
dinner was on the table. There was only one thing the matter
with it; the table was set with only eight places, and Mrs.
Hudson and the children were nowhere in sight.

When our family first moved to Colorado, back in 1906, there
had been five of us youngsters, about the ages of the Hudson
children. We were too poor to hire help, so Father worked for

the neighbors during haying, then they all came and helped us for the two or three days it took to get in our harvest. The rest of the year we lived pretty much on oatmeal, pork and beans, and johnnycake, but when the harvesters were coming Father went to town for a load of special groceries. Then Mother baked pies, and cakes, and raised white bread, while Father brought in a door from the bunkhouse, and built legs under it to make an extension for the table.

No matter how many neighbors came to help us, we all sat down at the table together—Mother at one end, with the baby in his high chair beside her, we youngsters next, then the neighbor men, and Father at the end opposite Mother. To us youngsters, those harvest meals seemed like extra Thanksgivings, and we looked forward to them as much as we did to Christmas.

A picture of the long table on the old ranch flashed into my head when I stepped into the kitchen that first Friday in harvest, stirring up a warm sort of memory. Maybe it was the door to the front room standing ajar, and my remembering that Father had used a door to extend the table, or maybe it was just knowing that Mrs. Hudson and the children were beyond that door. Before anyone had taken his seat, I called quietly, "Mrs. Hudson, may I speak to you a minute?"

When she came to the door there was a puzzled, half-frightened look on her face, as though she expected me to scold her about the dinner she'd cooked. I started out by telling her about our moving to Colorado because my father had tuberculosis, of how poor we were, and all the rest of the story, right down to how much we children looked forward to those harvest-time meals. Then I said, "I'd like to go back and do it all over again. Of course, I can't, but it would seem almost like the old days if you'd let us take that door off the hinges for extending this table, then you and the children would come and eat with us."

While I'd been telling the story she'd lost her half-frightened look, but it came back to her face when I mentioned their eating with us. "Oh, I couldn't do that," she said nervously.

"Joe, he's charged all the stuff to you . . . and besides . . . the younguns ain't used to strangers . . . they'd be scairt."

"We're not strangers any longer," I told her, "and we'll be around here until at least the end of the month, so they might just as well get acquainted now. As for the grub, we can't eat it till it's cooked, and it's pretty tough to spare Judy from the field to do the cooking. If you'll do it for us, your help will be worth a lot more than what you and the children can eat."

Really, we didn't miss Judy from the field very much when she went in to cook our meals. Either Gus or Lars could easily load a barge while the other drove the team, but there was no sense in letting Judy or her sister know it. Besides, I didn't want to give Mrs. Hudson time to think up any more excuses, so I said, "Gus, could you and Lars take that door down and set it up at the end of the table? You might bring in those boxes the canned stuff came in, Jaikus. They'll do for extra chairs till we have time to make another bench."

It took every odd dish, knife, fork, and spoon in the house to set the extended table, but with everyone helping it didn't take long to do it. When Mrs. Hudson brought the children from the front room they were clean, and still dressed in their town clothes, but they were all as timid as fawns. They clung tight to their mother and Judy, crowded away from us, and didn't look up as they passed. Judy was the one who eased things a bit. She took the two older girls by the hand, led them to the far end of the table, and told them, "We'll do it just like they done when Bud was a little boy. Your maw will sit on this end, with you girls next her on that side over there. Then will come Paco, but he don't talk no English, so you just help your-selves when he passes things. Billy can sit on this box, and then Susie, and then me, so's't I can cut her meat for her."

When we first sat down I thought I might have made a mis-take. Everyone, except Judy, seemed uncomfortable, and the children were just plain scared. They didn't dare help them-selves, but watched nervously as Judy and their mother served them, then they seemed afraid to touch the food, peeking up first toward their mother, and then toward Judy. The fellows, even Doc, seemed nearly as uncomfortable as Mrs. Hudson. They filled their plates in silence, and ate as if they weren't hungry. I had to do something to break the spell, so I asked Doc, "What do you think that forty we're working on will run; twenty bushels to the acre?"

"It might," he told me after a minute's thinking. "It just about might go twenty. The rest we've cut wouldn't make it."

That gave me the opening I needed. I looked down the table to Mrs. Hudson, and told her, "That doesn't mean that the crop will average out to less than twenty bushels. You see, we've been jumping around over both sections, harvesting the forties that were most apt to shatter. What we've cut so far was the driest and thinnest on the ground, so it will yield the least. I'm afraid some of it will go as little as twelve bushels to the acre. What do you think, Doc?"

"Might be," he told Mrs. Hudson, "but that's behind us now. I don't believe there's much left that won't run eighteen. Most of it looks to me like it would make the low twenties, some as much as twenty-five, and there are a few spots that will go as high as forty. Ought to average out a good full twenty."

Mrs. Hudson forgot her discomfort as soon as we began talking about the crop. "I'll bet I know some of them places that will run forty bushel," she told us. "There was patches on both these sections last year that was good enough to pay out for harvesting and thrashing, but the tenant figured that by the time he'd split with the owner he'd come out the loser, so he left it all stand. There was places I seen the seed laying thick on the ground when I disk . . ."

She cut off in the middle of the word, evidently not wanting us to know she'd done a good deal of the disking, so I asked "What type of wheat is this?"

"Turkey red," she told me. "Dark, hard Turkey red. The best there is. The owner furnished the seed for the tenant before us· paid a premium for it, over to the Oberlin Co-op."

I managed to get Lars and Gus into the conversation a bit

by asking them what kind of wheat was grown in Minnesota, when harvest time would begin there, and whether they used binders or headers. Even the children lost most of their uneasiness as soon the conversation began rolling. Their table manners weren't the best, and they often used fingers for forks, but once they got started they stowed the grub away in good shape, and Judy mothered them like a hen with a brood of chickens. "Them peas are a'most as good as if they come right out of a garden. Try some of 'em Marthy, you'll like 'em," or "Leave me cut that side meat for you, Sally. That old knife you've got is about as sharp on one end as it is on the other."

Before the meal was over I'd got Jaikus to tell us one of his stories about the old sod, and Old Bill to tell us how a man went about training a trotting horse for the race track. I could see that the older girls were listening to every word, but neither of them had ever looked toward our end of the table. I wanted to break the ice for them, but couldn't think how to do it until Old Bill told about training trotting horses. Every noon I'd been whittling away at my little wooden horse as we rested after dinner, and I'd finished it the previous noon. As soon as Bill had completed his story, I looked down the table, and asked, "Do you like horses, Marthy?"

She jumped as if I'd hurt her when I spoke her name, and Judy had to remind her that my question called for an answer. Still more than half frightened, Martha peeked at me, and said, "Not . . . not if they're ornery ones . . . that will tromp people."

"I've got one that will never tromp anybody," I told her, "because she can never get her feet off the ground. Her name is Fanny, and I used to ride her when I was about as old as you are, but she's only that tall." I held my fingers out to show about six inches, and asked, "Would you like to have her?"

The other fellows had seen me whittling, so they knew what I was talking about, but Judy, her sister, and the children looked as puzzled as if they thought I'd suddenly gone out of my mind. I let them puzzle a few seconds, and then told

Martha, "You won't be able to ride her, because she's whittled out of a stick of wood, but you might be able to make a harness for her with some string. Would you like to have her?"

Martha thought it over for a few seconds, peeked up again, and asked, "What would she cost? I got three pennies."

"All right," I told her. "You get me the three pennies and I'll go get old Fanny for you. That's just about what my old Fanny was worth, but I never had another horse I liked so much."

When I brought the little carving back from the barn the men were sitting in the shade beside the house and the children were clustered just inside the kitchen doorway. Judy and her sister had been clearing the table, but stopped to come and see what I'd brought. Martha forgot all about being afraid of me when she saw the little wooden horse. She almost danced a jig as she held her three pennies out, took the little piece in both hands, looked into its face, and rubbed its smooth back against one cheek.

Judy and her sister looked almost as excited as the children, and Judy asked in an awed voice, "Where'd you get her, Bud? How come you to bring her with you?"

"I didn't," I told her. "I whittled her out of an old chunk of two-by-six I found in the barn. I've whittled them ever since I was Marthy's age. When I get hold of a good piece of hardwood I'm going to carve one of a two-year-old gelding that's out in the pasture."

"That's Kitten's last colt," Mrs. Hudson told me, "and he's so ornery that even Myron couldn't do nothing with him. It's a pity he wasn't out of Vixen. He'd sure have made a fine colt, and not the killer kind neither."

Judy had already told me which of the horses were Kitten's colts, and which were Vixen's. Those from Vixen were larger, and inclined to slow down toward the end of a hard day. But those from Kitten never seemed to tire, never slowed down, and though they were manageable under careful handling, they never lost one spark of their fire. We'd been working the smallest pair of them full days on the header, because they were still too wild for barge use, and they were thriving on it. There would have been no sense in telling Mrs. Hudson that everything I liked in them had come straight from Kitten, so I just said, "Well, it's time we were getting back to work. Can I count on you to do the cooking for us, so we can have Judy full time in the field?"

"For my part, you sure can," she told me, "but you'll be getting the worst of the deal, what with five mouths to feed."

"It's the other way around," I told her. "I'll be way ahead by having all of Judy's time in the field." When I turned away they both looked as happy as the youngsters did with the little wooden horse.

9

New Fields to Reap

THE second break in our routine came at noon on our first Sunday. We'd just finished dinner, and were sitting in the shade of the house, when Bones drove into the yard and motioned me to him. "Looks like you been raising hob around here," he told me. "What did you do, put on some extra help?"

"No," I said, "I've got the same crew I started with."

"Thought I counted nineteen stacks as I drove in," he said. "How many acres do you aim to put into each one? Thrashers don't like it if you make 'em too small. Lose too much time in moving a rig from one stackyard to another."

"Twenty acres," I said. "Some of them may be a little small where the stand was light."

"Twenty acres!" he said, and scowled at me. "Do you know how big twenty acres is, Son?"

"Yes, sir," I told him, "an eighth by a quarter of a mile."

"Hmmf! That's right," he said, "but you haven't cut any three hundred and eighty acres."

"About three-ninety, as near as I can figure it," I told him, "but we've jumped around and cut the easiest stuff first."

That time he looked at me suspiciously, and demanded,

"What you doing that for? I won't let Clara pay you two dollars an acre unless you finish the whole job."

"I understand that," I told him; "it was part of our deal. We've been jumping around to catch the forties where the crop's the driest and most apt to shatter."

"Who told you to do that?" Bones asked, less brusquely.

"No one," I said, "but that's the way I'd do it if it were my own crop. We've cut a swath along each quarter-section line, so we have roadways, and don't knock down any standing grain when we move from one field to another."

"Well, I'll be doggoned!" he said with a big grin. "Thought you were a green horn in wheat country. Climb in and let's look about a bit. This old buggy's got a turned-up exhaust pipe, so we won't set a fire by driving through the fields."

With our having harvested forty-acre squares here and there on both sections, the whole place had somewhat the appearance of a new subdivision—the scattered stacks of yellow wheat looking like newly-built houses that hadn't yet been painted, and the swaths we'd cut between the forties marking off the streets. As Bones turned the car off the roadway and headed down the swath at the far end of the corral, he asked, "Where did you start harvesting? I'd like to take a look at the stuff."

"The forty at the corner of this section was first," I told him. "Hudson cut it, and took more straw than I've been taking. That's why the stacks are so much larger."

"Never mind that. Let's see the first one you cut," he said.

When we reached the forty we'd cut Monday forenoon, Bones wandered around it until he'd found a patch, maybe fifteen feet square, where I hadn't been quick enough in lowering the cutter bar. The straw was no more than eight inches tall, and before I could set the bar low enough I'd cut the heads in two, leaving the lower half on the stubble. I didn't want him to think I'd been wasting grain all week, so I said, "I was pretty green at running the header when we cut this forty, and the horses hadn't simmered down enough to pull steady. You won't find it so bad on the forties we've cut in the last few days."

"Where'd you learn to run a header?" he asked sharply.

"Over in that draw," I told him, pointing toward the hollow where we'd cut our horse feed. "The first few rounds look as if a blind man had cut it with a pair of dull sheep shears."

"I know what you mean," he said, "I've seen whole sections that looked the same way." He looked me up and down from head to foot, then said, "You're a light-weight for running a header. Don't you have any beefy man in the crew that could do it?"

"Yes," I told him, "three of them, but one's a better stacker than I am, and the other two are my best pitchers. Besides, I like to handle my own horses when they're working as hard as these header horses have to."

I caught myself as soon as I'd said, "my own horses," and Bones caught me, too. He grinned and said, "By the looks of things, they will be, so you might as well call 'em yours now. This patch of half-cut head doesn't worry me, but the stubble in this field does. You were changing the height of the cut every few feet, and heaving on a lift boom all day will strain the guts out of a big, stout man, leave alone a skinny kid. If you're set on doing the heading yourself, why don't you set the bar low enough to catch all the heads and let it go at that?"

"If I did that," I told him, "we'd have so much straw to handle that we couldn't cut more than forty acres a day, and the load on the horses would be too heavy. We've rigged the boom with a counterweight, so it's easy to raise and lower, and I've already toughened up enough that the job doesn't bother me."

"Hmmf! Looks like it," he said, "but I didn't come out here to tell you how to run your job. I came to see how much shattering there'd been, and to get some idea of what Clara might hope to get out of her crop. I can't see much shattering on this forty."

"No, this one wasn't bad," I told him, "but there's one that was. We should have taken it right after this one, but didn't get at it till Thursday. With this hot wind blowing, I'm afraid there's a good deal of it on the ground. Every time a barge was unloaded the floor would be red with grain."

"How many more you had like that?" he asked quickly.

"None," I said, "and I don't think we'll have any more. I have a man here who knows wheat pretty well, and we've been watching ahead more closely since Thursday."

"Let's take a look at that bad one," Bones said, and hurried back to the car.

He spent maybe ten minutes walking around that forty. "Not bad," he said at last. "Not enough on the ground to make seed for next year. If this is the worst you strike, Clara's going to be in luck. Let's take a look at the stacks."

The two stacks on that forty were the smallest we had. Bones examined them as though he were looking for a bird's nest, then grabbed a handful, and asked, "You Scotch?"

"Some of my folks were," I told him.

"Thought so! You're sure stingy with the straw you take."

"Did you see any cut heads left in this field?" I asked.

"No. No," he said, "but you've sure got these heads skinned off tight. The thrasher's going to like this. He'll get danged near as much wheat as straw out of these stacks."

"I don't think so," I told him. "The kernels on this forty ran pretty small, and they weren't well filled out."

He laid a wheat head on one palm, rubbed it with the other, and blew the chaff away, then stepped back, evidently trying to gage the size of the stacks. "Hmmf! Won't run over twelve bushel to the acre," he said, with the corner of his mouth turned down.

"That's what my man, Doc, figured it would run," I told him.

"Must be a good man," he said, "knows his wheat all right. What does he figure the whole crop will average?"

"A shade better than twenty bushels to the acre," I said.

"Doubt it! Doubt it'll come close. Not from what I've seen so far. Let's go look at the rest of it."

We spent more than two hours, going to each stack, and wading through the uncut grain on each forty. Bones must have rubbed a thousand heads of wheat on his palms, blown

the chaff away, then examined the kernels. By the time we left each field or pair of stacks, he'd tell me what he thought that forty would average. Then, when we were through and had started back toward the house, he said, "That man of yours is all right. I'd go along with his guess that both sections will average out a good full twenty bushels to the acre."

"What is wheat bringing this year?" I asked.

"Dollar ninety-eight at the elevator yesterday," he told me. "That's for number one, dark, hard; and most of what's still standing will run number one. The rest will run number two, at about a dollar ninety."

I didn't say any more, because I was doing a little figuring, and Bones knew it. "Working it out in your head?" he asked.

"Roughly," I said. "If I've figured right, it's about a fifty-thousand-dollar crop."

"Not for Clara," he told me. "As near as I can find out—what with interest, and court costs, and one thing and another— Hudson was in the hole about nine thousand. Then half the crop will go to the owner, and there'll be the harvesting, and thrashing, and hauling her share; that'll run up to maybe six thousand, so, if all goes well, she could come out with ten thousand clear. That would leave her raise those children in town, where they could go to a good school. Might do more than that for her. There's many a good man, ones who would make those little kids a mighty fine father, that wouldn't back away from a widow woman with ten thousand in the bank."

I wasn't a bit surprised to hear that Hudson had been nine thousand dollars in the hole, but the figure of six thousand for getting the crop harvested, thrashed, and half of it hauled to the elevator seemed way out of line. I turned it over in my head a couple of times, then said, "Thrashing must be pretty expensive around here, or you must be off on your figure of six thousand. The harvesting will cost only twenty-five hundred and sixty."

"It's not the harvesting or thrashing," he told me; "it's the hauling. It's a good eight miles to the elevator, and it costs a cent and a half a bushel a mile to get wheat hauled—that is, if you get a hauler that will keep up with the machine. Of course, a man can dump it on the ground, and haul it himself when he has time, but only a fool would do that. Too much chance of getting it rained on, lots of extra work to scooping it up again, and the elevator will dock you at least a dime a bushel if there's any dirt in it."

For the last several days I'd been trying to figure out what I'd do with the horses when harvest was over, and I thought maybe I'd found the answer. By doing a little arithmetic in my head, I came up with a figure slightly over three thousand dollars for hauling the crop from those two sections. I went over the arithmetic a second time, then asked, "Do most of the owners who lease out their land hire their share of the crop hauled?"

"Sure!" he told me, half irritably. "How would they haul it themselves? Most of 'em live in Denver, Omaha, or Kansas City."

I waited another minute, and said, "I suppose you know most of the owners . . . and their addresses."

"A few," he said, "but the place to get that kind of information is from the County Clerk, over to Oberlin." Then he suddenly saw through what I was driving at, grinned, and said, "Aiming to put those little broncos to work when harvest is over, eh?"

"Could be," I said, grinning back.

"Well," he said, "you'll have both hands full to do the hauling from this place, and Clara'll want you to do it. It'll take four of those little broncs to haul a fifty-bushel load over these roads, and they can't make more than two trips a day from this far out."

"How long does the thrashing season run?" I asked him.

"About two months," he told me.

"And how long should it take for the job on this place?" I asked.

"Maybe three weeks," he said. "What you getting at?"

"Well," I said, "that would give me a chance to do a good

deal of hauling for other owners before and after this job, wouldn't it?"

"Hmmf! That's right," he said. "Hadn't thought of that. I'll write to a couple of owners for you in the morning, but don't bite off more than you can chew."

I barely had time to thank Bones before we reached the house, then he went in to talk with Mrs. Hudson, and I went to our camp behind the barn. It was already so late there was little use in going back to the field, so I told the crew, "Let's take the rest of the day off. We're far enough ahead that I'm not worried about finishing by the end of the month, and if I give the header a good overhauling today we might get through another week without a breakdown. You fellows take it easy and get some rest."

By supper time I had the old header in pretty good shape again, and as I worked I had lots of time to think about going into the wheat hauling business.

The next week rolled along as though we'd been living and harvesting together all our lives. I think Mrs. Hudson liked her place at the end of the table, and we liked her cooking. The children, and even the dogs, lost their fear, and each day we put more than fifty acres of wheat in the stacks.

Every noon of that week Judy gave me a lesson in driving the old Maxwell, so I'd be able to make hurry-up trips to Oberlin when we had a breakdown and needed repair parts. It's a good thing that she took me out to the middle of a stubble field for my first lesson. There was a half-turn play in the steering wheel, I always turned it too far and too fast, and the more trouble I had in steering the harder I was inclined to push down on the gas pedal. It probably came from my boyhood habit of bracing my feet against the dashboard when I had to pull on the reins. Whatever it came from, it didn't work worth a dime. Anyone seeing that field from a distance would have though there was a dustdevil whirling through it, and I'll swear there were times when the old Maxwell was spinning as fast.

Some of the lessons lasted a full hour, so I had plenty of time to tell Judy about my plan to go into the wheat hauling business. And she had time to tell me what a good place Beaver Valley would be for a man to go into the cattle business.

Judy and I never did any spooning, but her sister wouldn't let her help with the dishes, so there wasn't much for either of us to do right after supper. And it was sort of restful to walk up the lane to the pasture and back in the first cool breeze of evening—just walking along slowly, and watching the stars come out, and talking about hauling wheat or the cattle business.

10

Bamboozling Bones

By the end of our second week we were so far along that there was no doubt of our finishing the harvest with time to spare. When we were unharnessing Saturday noon I asked the crew, "How would you like to take this afternoon off and go to Oberlin? There's a barber shop over there that has baths, and I've got some business to take care of with the County Clerk."

It didn't take the men two seconds to make up their minds, and by one o'clock we were on our way. Doc sat beside me, all rigged out in his medicine-man clothes, and the crazy part of it was that he'd put on his medicine-man behavior and talk right along with the clothes. Instead of calling me Bud, he called me, "My dear companion," and he couldn't open his mouth without orating. Worse than that, he couldn't keep it closed.

The main street at Oberlin was crowded with Saturday shoppers, and though I could keep the old Maxwell on the road fairly well, I didn't trust myself to try parking it in any tight spot. I turned off on a side street, parked where there was plenty of room, then told the fellows, "I brought the checkbook along, and you can draw whatever you'd like, up to a hundred dollars apiece."

Jaikus and Old Bill said five dollars would be enough, Gus and Lars just shook their heads, but Doc began rubbing his hands together excitedly. With a sweep of his arm back toward the main street, he orated, "My dear companion, Fortune stretches forth her golden arms to embrace us. Yonder throng eagerly awaits the boon of Doctor J. Holloway Merriweather's famous Elixir of Longevity. Shall it be denied these good people? Ah, no! You and I will procure from the local apothecary certain chemicals, spirits, and appropriate bottles, repair to the seclusion of some babbling brook, and . . ."

"You do the repairing, Doc," I told him. "I'll be busy all afternoon. Just tell me how much to make your check for."

"Oh, fifty will suffice," he told me grandly. "A mere pittance, but 'twill suffice to establish a lucrative enterprise."

I'd no sooner written the check than Doc grabbed it, backed out of the old Maxwell, bowed to us, and announced, "Fortune awaits me, gentlemen. I shall rejoin you anon." Then he hurried away toward the main street.

"Well, make the rejoining no later than six o'clock," I called after him, "if you haven't already been run out of town by that time. I promised we'd be back for supper and to do the milking."

Gus, Lars, Jaikus, and Old Bill decided to get haircuts and baths, then go see a movie, and Paco wanted to stay with me. I could hardly take him, so as we walked back to the corner I told him what the others were going to do, gave him two dollars, and said I thought it would be better if he went along with them. After I'd shown them where the barber's shop with bath rooms was, I stopped at a drug store, bought a pad of writing paper and two dozen envelopes, then asked where I'd find the County Clerk's office.

The Clerk took it for granted that I wanted to lease a place on shares when I told him I'd like to look up the names and addresses of absentee owners of wheat land in the northwestern part of the country. At first he acted a little crusty, and told me he didn't know of any owners in Beaver Valley who weren't satisfied with the tenants they already had. But when I told him what I was planning to do, and that I could give the banker in Cedar Bluffs as my reference, he became more than obliging. He gave me maps of half a dozen townships, showing each piece of property and the owner's name. There wasn't a piece of land on those maps that he didn't know, and he outlined in red pencil the ones that had absentee owners and were planted to wheat. Then he looked up the addresses for me, and wrote them on the maps, along with the names of the tenants.

It was nearly three o'clock before I'd thanked the Clerk for his kindness, and left his office. From there I went to the post office, where there were pens, ink, and a high desk to write at. I had to make three or four fresh starts, and it took me at least half an hour to write the first letter, telling the owner that I had been referred to him by the Decatur County Clerk, that I was equipped to transport grain from his property to the elevator as rapidly as it was thrashed, that my charge would be ten and a half cents a bushel, and that he could assure himself of my honesty and reliability by communicating with the First State Bank of Cedar Bluffs. After I'd signed my name I remembered that most advertising letters had a hooker at the end, so I added a P.S. "I reserve the right to decline any order, and can accept none received later than August 10, 1919."

After that first one, the letters took only a few minutes apiece, because the only difference was in the price per bushel. I figured that out by looking at the maps to count the number of miles from the property to the nearest railroad town, then multiplied it by one and a half. It made the letters sound more personal than if I'd written, "a cent and a half per bushel per mile." Then I put special delivery stamps on the envelopes to make them look more important.

There was no sense in trying to write to every owner whose address the County Clerk had given me, so I picked out the twenty-three with property ten miles or less from the railroad. It was nearly six o'clock when I finished my letters to the land owners, then I scribbled a note to my mother, telling her where I was, and that I was feeling fine. Just before the post office closed, I bought a penny postal card, addressed it to my older sister, Grace, and wrote on it, "Have found a nickel bush, and am shaking it." I knew she'd understand what it meant, for when we were kids and found an easy way of making a little money we'd always tell each other that we'd found a nickel bush.

The crew was waiting at the Maxwell when I got there, all except Doc, but no one had seen him. I'd been on the main street enough that I'd have noticed if he'd gathered a crowd there for a medicine pitch, so could only guess that he was making it on some side street. After waiting fifteen or twenty minutes, we drove all around the main part of town, but there was no sign of Doc or a crowd that he might have drawn. There was only one thing left to do, so I parked the car again, and we spread out to hunt for Doc. It was Old Bill who found him. "Doc's down to the pool hall," he told me, "sleeping on a row of chairs, and he smells like he's been into the tanglefoot."

Although I'd guessed that Doc might hit the bottle if he had a chance, I hadn't worried about his doing it in Oberlin, because Kansas was a bone-dry state. But if he'd ever gone to a local apothecary for chemicals, spirits, and bottles, he'd come away with only the spirits. He was completely out, with a half-empty bottle of moonshine peeping from the pocket of his frock coat. With Lars to help me, we sat him up, stashed his bottle, put his hat on his head, and got him to his feet. He was docile as an old sheep till we had him standing, then he threw his chest out and his head back, like a rooster getting ready to crow. With one sweep of his arm he sent me flying, rose to his toes, and bellowed, "Gentlemen, I have a purpose! Show me a man without a purpose, and I will show you . . ."

Right at that point Doc ran out of wind—and control of his legs. Gus and Lars draped his arms around their shoulders, and carried him, legs dragging helplessly, to the car. Most of the way his head hung as though his neck were broken, but a couple of times he raised it enough to blubber, "Gen'lmen I have a pursos . . ." We poured him onto the floor in the back of the Maxwell, and the fellows held him down with their feet on the way home.

When I shook Doc awake next morning he didn't know anything about our having brought him home from town, or what had happened to his fifty dollars, but he did know that he'd had part of a bottle of moonshine left. His eyes were swollen and bloodshot, he held onto his head with both hands, and told me, "I'm an awful sick man, Bud, an awful sick man. I was taken with one of my seizures right after I left you boys. Might have died if I hadn't got hold of some medicine for it. Lucky I saved enough to get me back on my feet again. Fetch it for me, will you, Bud? It's in the pocket of my coat."

"No, it isn't," I told him, "but you've still got enough of it in you to float a rowboat. Roust out of that blanket and pull your overalls on; it's nearly sunrise."

"Aw, Bud," he wailed, "you didn't heave that bottle out, did you? I'll never make it through the day without a hair of the dog. I'm apt to be laid up for a week."

"I'll make you a bet," I told him. "If you're not ready to go by the time we start for the field, you'll have another seizure —and Gus and Lars will do the seizing. They lugged you to the car last night, and they can lug you as far as our next stack. Haul those britches on and get a quart of milk into you; that'll put out some of the fire." Doc made it, but the stacks he built looked as though they had about as much hangover as he did.

By Monday morning Doc had worked off the effects of his seizure, and for the next four days we poured wheat into the stacks at a faster clip than we'd ever reached before. Then, about the middle of Friday forenoon, I looked up to see Bones driving across the stubble field. He was coming so fast that his car bounced like a running rabbit, he swung it in a half-circle, pulled alongside the header, and slammed on the brake. Before I could stop the horses, he shouted, "What in Sam Hill have you been up to? I'm getting letters from all over, wanting to know how much hauling equipment you own, and if you're reliable."

"Good!" I said. "What are you telling them?"

"Telling 'em!" he barked. "What can I tell 'em? Unless you get this job finished by the end of the month you won't own anything but the clothes on your back."

"That's right," I told him, "but today is only the 25th, and there are only six more forties to harvest. We could make it by the end of the month if we all had one hand tied behind us."

"And what will you have if you do make it?" he shouted. "A bunch of runty little broncs that wouldn't bring ten dollars apiece, and a couple of worn-out old wagons. How you going to haul wheat with any such outfit as that? Leastways, more than has to be hauled from this place, and you gave Clara your word on that."

"Right again," I said, "except that there will be three worn-out wagons. Did Mrs. Hudson tell you she's promised the thrashing job to the man with the biggest rig anywhere around here?"

"Well, what of that?" he asked.

"Only this," I told him: "I've promised her I'd haul both her share and the landlord's as fast as it was thrashed, and they've given me the job."

"Then what you messing around trying to get all these outside jobs for?" he asked angrily. "With no more horses and wagons than you've got, you'll have both hands full and your britches to hold up if you keep your promise to Clara."

"That's more than right," I told him. "How much will that big rig thrash in a day—in wheat headed as tight as this is?"

"About fourteen hundred bushel a day," he told me.

"That's about what I figured," I said. "If you're not in too big a hurry, let's do some arithmetic. The crew could stand a little rest this hot morning."

As I said it I motioned Paco to watch the header horses, climbed down from my perch, took a screwdriver from the tool box, and scraped a patch of ground smooth with one foot. "What you up to now?" Bones asked irritably.

"A little arithmetic," I told him. "I might make some mistakes, so come and help me, will you?"

We both knelt by the patch I'd scraped bare, with me holding the screwdriver as though it were a pencil. "Now this is the way it looks to me," I said. "I'll have twelve horses and three wagons, and if I remember right, you told me I couldn't haul more than fifty bushels to a load, or make more than two round trips a day from this far out."

"Well?" Bones asked.

Putting down the figures with the screwdriver, I said, "That's two trips a day for three wagons, equals six, times fifty bushels, equals three hundred, and you say the rig will thrash fourteen hundred a day."

"Hmmf! Hmmf!" he sniffed. "Well, Clara'll have to find herself some more haulers, or I'll have to find 'em for her."

"No," I told him, "the job is mine and I'll do my own finding —that is, unless you want to give me some help with it. You tell me these horses are worth only ten dollars apiece; what would it cost me to buy some more just like them?"

"Nobody but Hudson would waste pasture on this kind of wild cayuses," he told me. "But, what with harvest about over, a man might pick up some nags for around a hundred dollars a pair."

"And how much for secondhand harness and wagons?" I asked.

"Oh," he said, "I guess you could pick up some pretty fair harness for around fifty a set, and if you took wagons that needed some fixing up, you might get 'em for somewhere around thirty."

"Fine," I said. "How much a day would it cost me to hire a good pair of horses and a wagon that wouldn't need fixing up?"

Bones scowled at me, and said, "Don't know. There's no call around here for renting 'em out. County allows three dollars a team for working out road taxes. What in blazes are you trying to scare up outside hauling for, when you've got to hire teams and wagons to haul what's on this place. Why don't you use your head?"

"That's what I'm trying to do," I told him. "And that's why I think it would be better to buy horses and wagons than to rent them. If your estimate of two trips with fifty bushels to the load is right, I'll need eleven more wagons and sixteen more horses to handle fourteen hundred bushels a day."

He sprang to his feet, and said, "Well, there's no sense wasting any more time in talking about it. The job's way too big for you, Son. Even if you had the price of eleven more hauling rigs, you'd be a fool to buy 'em. The investment would be way too big for the return. I'd never lend you the money. You haul what you can for Clara with what you've got—or will have—and I'll line up haulers to handle the rest of it."

"No, sir," I told him. "It's my job and I'm going to handle it all, and a good deal more besides—that is, if you don't kick things over for me by telling owners I'm not dependable."

Bones put a hand on my shoulder, and spoke as though I were his little boy and he was breaking the news about Santa Claus. "Son," he told me, "there's nothing I like any better than to see a boy trying to get ahead, but you've got to learn to walk before you run. Sure, you've done a fine job on this harvesting, better than I'd have believed you could do, but what's the sense in throwing away what you've already made. If you'd try tackling a job such as you're talking about, you'd only go broke again— and leave every owner that gave you a hauling job in a jackpot. A man's got to figure things out before he jumps into 'em whole-hog."

"That's why I brought this screwdriver," I told him, "but I sometimes make mistakes in arithmetic, so I'd appreciate it if you'd watch while I figure it over again. First, let's figure what the hauling from this place would bring in. There are 1280 acres in two sections, times twenty bushels to the acre, equals 25,600 bushels, times twelve cents, equals $3,072. We'll put that down over on this side. Then sixteen horses at a hundred dollars a team would be $800. Eight sets of harness at fifty would be $400. Eleven wagons at thirty dollars each would come to $330, and let's figure that labor and material to rebuild them would cost another $200. That would make a total investment of $1730. Is that right so far?"

Bones nodded, so I went on, "Now we'll divide 25,600 by 1400, and that gives us eighteen, the number of days it should take to thrash the crop on this place."

"What good does it do you to know that?" Bones asked.

"I have to know it before I can figure the cost of labor, grub, and horse feed," I told him. "I'm planning to use my wagons in pairs, with a four-horse hitch, and haul a hundred bushels to each trip."

"You'll never make it!" Bones told me sharply. "You've got two deep gulches between here and town. Four of these little broncos couldn't pull more than seventy bushels out of either one."

"I've looked them over and I think you're right," I told him, "so I plan to use an extra team of heavy tote horses at each of those gulches. If six of these little broncs can pull this fifteen-foot header, can't four of them haul a hundred bushels the rest of the way to town?"

"Reckon so," he said, irritably, "but get on with your figuring; I got other fish to fry."

"All right," I told him. "Let's see what it will cost for overhead and labor. A man can hire pretty good drivers for seven dollars a day, can't he?"

"The best," he told me.

"Then let's put down six drivers at seven dollars a day—I'll drive one of the rigs myself. That's seven time six is $42, and we'll say the two heavy tote teams I'll hire will cost another ten. That makes $52. Grub and horse feed might run as much as twenty dollars a day, making a daily total of $72, times 18 days, equals $1,296. Now we'll add that to the $1,730 it will cost for new horses and equipment, and it equals $3,026, but I'll take in $3,072 on the hauling from these two sections alone. On all the other hauling jobs I get, I'll make . . ."

Bones saw through it before I was quite finished, and jumped to his feet as if a firecracker had exploded under him. "Get on with your work, Son! Get on with your work! No sense leaving your crew stand around idle," he told me as he climbed back into his car. "I'll let you have two thousand dollars for thirty days—at eight percent, you understand. And I'll get the answers to those letters off on the noon train."

He started to drive away, then stopped and shouted, "I'll get right to work, rounding up horses, harness, and wagons for you."

"That's fine," I called back, "but don't make any deals till I see the stuff, and I won't have time to look at it before the middle of next week."

I hadn't done my arithmetic for Bones the same as I'd done it for myself, but in the way that I thought would save the most arguments and do the best job of selling. I knew my tough little mustangs well enough to be sure they could travel ten miles a day farther than he would have believed, so I'd be able to haul thirty per cent more wheat per horse than we'd figured on. And with that extra thirty per cent, I could easily afford to pay my crew ten dollars a day instead of seven. Then too, I'd figured that the new horses and equipment would cost me nearly $2,500, instead of the $1,730 we'd used in our arithmetic. But I'd let Bones name the prices I'd probably have to pay, and there was no sense in telling him I thought he was too low.

Old Bill's barge had been at the header while Bones and I were talking, and I was sure that Jaikus had understood only enough to be completely confused, but he was a babbler, and I didn't want him to get the crew upset. So, as I climbed back onto the header, I called out, "I don't want any talking about this until after we've had dinner. Then I'll tell all of you what I plan to do, and any of you who want to can go along on the deal."

For the past couple of weeks every mealtime had been a happy time, with everyone talking and joking, but that noon what little conversation there was seemed forced. I waited until everyone had finished eating, then looked up at Mrs. Hudson and asked, "Do you think you could put up with us for another month or two, on the same kind of deal we've had during harvest?"

Martha didn't give her mother a chance to answer, but cut in excitedly, "Sure we will, won't we Maw? Me and Sally'll do all the dishes for you, like we done this past week, and Susie can look after Billy and the baby."

Mrs. Hudson spanked her hands together, and said, "Quiet! Sure we'll do it, and it's kindly of Bud to ask us, but hush up and let him talk."

"I'd better do a little asking first," I said. "How about the rest of you? Want to stick around and put up with me for a boss a while longer, if I can promise you ten dollars a day in wages?"

Although Paco couldn't understand the words, he had a good idea of what I was talking about, and nodded vigorously when the others all said they wanted to stay. I'd been pretty sure they would, for with harvest just about over, there'd be only two kinds of jobs for hired hands in that country; general farm work at about fifty dollars a month, or pitching wheat on a thrashing crew at six or seven dollars a day.

Judy didn't answer when the others did, but tried to act as if she were so busy cutting Billy's meat that she hadn't heard me. "How about you, Judy?" I asked. "If this scheme works out as well as I hope it will, we'll be hauling more wheat than any outfit in this part of the county, and I'll need your help."

She peeked up at me, and said, "I'd like to, Bud. You know that. But it wouldn't be fitting—a girl driving a wheat wagon . . . through town and all."

"I couldn't afford to have you driving a wheat wagon," I told her. "I'll need someone who knows every wheat farmer living within ten miles of The Bluffs, and who can go around to find out when they're going to have their thrashing done, and what sized rigs will be used. Besides, I'll need you to keep my books."

"Well," she said, "I know all the wheat farmers . . . or mostly all, but I didn't never keep no books."

"That makes no difference," I told her. "Nobody else ever kept books the way we're going to keep them. What do you say? Going to stick with the crew?"

"If you want me," she said, as happy as Martha had been. Then she added, "Leastways, I'll stay up till school commences, but I wouldn't be worth no . . ."

I didn't let her go any further, but began telling about having sent out letters to land owners, and what I planned about extra horses, harness, and wagons if we got enough jobs, and how I believed we could do the hauling best. When I'd finished, I said, "Of course, Bill and Jaikus heard all this when I was having my wrangle with the banker this forenoon, except that the figures were a little different, and I guess they thought I was out of my mind."

"Still think so," Bill broke in. "What you going to pay that robber eight per cent interest for, when you know we won't be drawing much of anything, and you'll have all the money you need right on your checkbook?"

"Because most of that money belongs to you fellows, not to me," I told him.

Paco was the only one who didn't tell me to use the money as if it were all my own, and the only reason he didn't tell me was because he didn't understand what we were talking about.

"You make me awfully proud and happy," I told them, "but you see it's like this; when you go fishing for bullheads you use angleworms, but when you go fishing for bankers you use interest. Bones is already charging Mrs. Hudson eight per cent on the amount he's credited to my account, but there isn't any real money in there; it's only a credit. No money will go out of his bank until I spend it for horses and wagons, and if he can charge me another eight per cent he'll make a nice fat profit. We wouldn't get many outside hauling jobs unless he sent out letters saying we'd do a good job, and the only reason for his doing it is to make the profit. Eight per cent interest on two thousand dollars for thirty days will cost only thirteen thirty-three, and that's cheap enough for getting set up in a new business. But right now, we'd better think about finishing the job we're on."

With the crew knowing what my plans were, no one—except Doc—wanted to knock off to go to town that week end, and I never saw any crew work harder in the field. By working until dark on Wednesday, July 30th, we put the last of Mrs. Hudson's harvest in the stacks—a full day ahead of schedule. But we weren't the only ones who were ahead of schedule. When I'd sent out the letters to land owners I'd put down Hudson's R.F.D. box number as my address, and by the time we'd finished the harvest I had half a dozen orders for hauling wheat. The only real trouble was that they were widely scattered over three townships.

11

Haggling and Horses

THERE is always a border around the outside of wheat fields, where the barge horses have trampled down the grain. On the Hudson place the border was weedy enough that I didn't think it should go into the stacks, but it would make pretty fair horse feed. The morning after we finished harvesting I stopped after breakfast to talk to Mrs. Hudson about the border and a few other things I had in mind. Until then the horses had been hers, and she had to furnish the feed for them, but that morning I gave her a check for $300 and they became mine, so I had to feed them.

After I'd given her the check, I said, "Now I'd like to make a deal with you, if you think it's a fair one. Judy tells me you have a quarter section planted in corn. I don't know much about corn in this part of the country, but if it were anywhere that I've ever farmed it would need cultivating once a month."

"Not here," she told me. "All that corn will need from now till shucking time is one good working with a weeder-cultivator. It's best if you can do it right after a rain, but if you don't have no rain you go ahead and do it anyways . . . and hope for the best."

137

"Well, then the deal I was going to make you would be lop-sided," I told her. "I'm going to have to find feed for these horses, and pasture for any I'm not using. What I was going to offer was to cultivate that corn for you in exchange for the use of the pasture, and for whatever feed there is in the border around the fields, but that wouldn't be a fair deal with only one cultivating."

"It would be more than fair to me," she said. "I couldn't get nothing for the pasture or that border, and it would cost me a couple of hundred dollars to get the corn cultivated. I'd be obliged to you if you wanted to deal that way."

I told her I'd be more than glad to, and I was. With that border being about twenty feet wide and eight miles long, there would be a bit more than thirteen acres of combination hay and grain in it—enough to feed my horses all the rest of the summer and fall.

Although we could harvest fifty acres of wheat in a day, the cutting of that border was slow and tricky business, and some of the hauls to the corral were more than two miles long, so it took us all forenoon to do our haying. By that time the mailman had brought me four more letters, each of them a hauling order.

After dinner I set Gus and Lars to taking the wagons apart for rebuilding, and the rest of the fellows to taking the con-veyors off the header, clearing up the yard, and getting things shipshape around the place, then I had Judy drive me to The Bluffs. I already had orders enough to know I'd be safe in buying the extra horses and equipment I'd need for the hauling business, but I thought it would be best to let Bones see the letters.

He came hurrying across the street from his house as we pulled up in front of the bank, and as he came he called to me, "Got three letters on my desk for you, Son. Thought you'd want me to open 'em up, so I did. Every one of 'em's a go-ahead for wheat hauling, and I've been right busy, getting all the stuff you'll need lined up for you. Come on in." He kept right on talking as I followed him to his desk: "I've got it all laid out on a map, so you'll know right where to go, and what to get at each place. Had to haggle some of 'em right down to the bone, but I got you some awful good buys—stuff you couldn't touch yourself for twice the price—but I know all these farmers, and which ones are pressed a mite for cash."

The map he'd drawn covered nearly half the top of his desk, took in a radius of about ten miles around the town, and he'd marked out a route for me to follow. Here and there along it, he'd outlined a place in red pencil, printed the farmer's name, and listed the items I'd buy from him, together with the prices. The first thing that caught my eye was that all the prices were about ten per cent higher than those he'd given me when we'd had our talk in the wheat field. I didn't mention it, but folded the map, tucked it under the belt of my jeans, and said, "I'm much obliged to you, and I'll go look at some of this stuff this afternoon. You didn't make any set deals on any of it, did you?"

"No. Not *set* deals, you understand. Just did the haggling for you, and told 'em you'd be around to pick up the stuff. You wouldn't be able to do much good on any but the stuff I've marked down for you, and from those I've named on the map."

As he spoke, he pulled a paper from a pigeonhole, laid it on the desk, and pushed it toward me. It was about the size of a check, with my name and $2000 typed on the top line. Just below it was, "8% All goods and chattels," then a couple of inches of real fine printing, and a blank line at the bottom. "Made the note up so we wouldn't have to fuss around with it after you came in," he said. "You sign there on the bottom line."

"No, I don't either," I told him. "If you want to make out a straight note for two thousand dollars, for thirty days, at eight per cent, with your security being whatever chattels I may buy with the two thousand, then I'll sign it. If you don't want that kind of a note, we'll forget about the loan, and I'll buy what I need from the money that's already in my account."

"Hmf! Hmf! This is a straight note," he said irritably; "the kind we use on all our loans."

"That's all right," I told him. "I don't care what kind of notes other people sign, but I don't sign any with fine print on them. We'll just forget about the loan."

"Now, now, Son!" he said. "A loan was a part of our deal."

"That's right," I said, "and I'm still willing to make it, but only if the note is made out as I just told you."

"Well," he said, "I suppose people do things different in different parts of the country, and we don't see many Easterners around here. If you'd rather have a note written out on a blank form I can do that all right; it'll only take a minute."

He took a blank I PROMISE TO PAY note from another pigeonhole, and I watched him as he filled it out, but I didn't tell him it would be the first note I'd ever signed. After he'd filled it out the right way, I signed it, and he made out a deposit slip. Then we shook hands, and I told him I'd go to look at some of the stuff he'd lined up for me.

While I'd been in the bank Judy had gone to Joe's store to pick up some more fresh meat, eggs, and a few other things we needed. After I'd helped her lug the groceries out to the Maxwell, I showed her the map, and said, "Let's not follow the route Bones laid out for us. We couldn't get halfway around it this afternoon, and it would leave us too far from home at supper time. Pick out a few that we might hit without going too far out of our way."

The more Judy studied the map the more puzzled she looked. "I declare," she said at last, "it looks like Bones is sending you to everybody's poor relations. None of these he's wrote down are wheat farmers, leastways they don't have more'n a little patch, and maybe some corn. They're all cow people, and the no-accountest ones anywheres around."

"Well, what's the matter with that?" I asked her. "That's the kind of people who would be most apt to have the kind of stuff I want to buy; stuff that won't cost too much. Let's go take a look."

The first place we went to was only a few miles from town,

on the break of the steep hills leading up to the high divide.
The house was a dugout, built into the hillside. There were a
couple of ramshackle sheds, a barbed-wire corral with a few
scrubby horses in it, and beyond that some scrubby looking
cattle grazed in a rough, gulch-torn pasture. The man wasn't
at home, but his wife came out to the car, and when I told her
what I'd come for she pointed toward the corral, and told me,
"Them two bays on the far side. Fred said to tell you the price
was a hundred and ten dollars."

I didn't get out of the car. From where I sat I could see that
the two bays were probably twice as old as I, that they were as
skinny as sawhorses, and on their last legs. If my broncos
weren't worth more than ten dollars apiece, those two old
plugs together weren't worth fifty cents. I thanked the lady
for her trouble, and told her I might drop back some time when
her husband was at home, then we drove on to the next place.

It was a bit more prosperous looking than the first, but not
much, and under the name Bones had written: "One team
horses $112.50. One Studebaker wagon $35. Two sets harness
$109.75."

At that place the man was at home, and though he had no
idea he was doing it, he saved me a lot of time and trouble.
The horses he showed me were about like my own bay mares;
good enough for ordinary farm work, but getting old and slow.
The harness was good enough for what I needed, but priced
way too high, and the wagon was in the same shape Hudson's
had been when I first saw them. After I'd looked the harness
and wagon over carefully, I told the man, "Your horses aren't
the kind I need, but I could use the wagon and harness if you
want to take a right price for them. I'll give you twenty dollars for the wagon, and seventy-five for the two sets of harness."

"Well," he said slowly, "I'd like awful well to let you have
'em, but Bones, he won't leave me take no less than them
prices he wrote down on the map."

I didn't have to be very smart to see through the whole
thing in less than a second. "That's okay," I told him. "I'll drop

in and have a talk with Bones. If we can get together on a price, I'll pick up the wagon and harness the first of the week."

The man seemed quite happy, so we shook hands, and I went out to the road where Judy was waiting in the Maxwell. "Back to the bank," I told her. "There's no sense in trying to fish with the wrong end of the pole in my hands. Now I know why we were sent to the poor relations, and I'm going to have some mighty poor relations with Bones if he tries this kind of a trick on me again."

From the time I was old enough to swap jackknives, I'd always been in some kind of dicker, and had often come out at the little end of the horn. But when I got stuck it was usually because I'd run into someone who was more clever at deceiving than I was at misleading. The line between misleading and deceiving isn't very wide, but to me it had always seemed that a man was cheating if he went over it. I'd misled Bones in my arithmetic, and my hollering about the small print on the note was done to mislead him on my age, but I hadn't deceived him. I would have if I'd told him I was twenty-one, making the note I'd signed collectible in court.

Even at that, I didn't mind if the other fellow tried to do a little deceiving in a dicker. It was to be expected, and made it more fun to match wits against him. What made me sore was having Bones try to bunko me into thinking that he was dickering on my side when he was actually my opponent. I'd have boiled over if I'd walked into the bank right after leaving that farmer, but I had time to simmer down before we got back to The Bluffs.

Bones was talking on the phone when I went in. I waited until he'd hung up, then opened the gate and went back to his desk. He seemed surprised when he looked up and saw me, cracked a couple of knuckles, and asked, "Something more I can do for you, Son?"

"No," I told him, "you've done more than enough already. I just dropped in to bring back this map. I won't be needing it; I'm going to buy my stuff at Oberlin."

Bones scowled at me, angrily, "Now wait a minute, Son! I went to a lot of trouble on your account, running down all that stuff for you, and haggling over prices. I don't aim to . . ."

"Neither do I," I cut in. "Just because I pulled you out of the hole on your worthless loans to Hudson is no reason for expecting me to pull you out on all the rest of them. I'll buy what I need from men who are free to do their own trading; not from dupes for a banker who has already foreclosed on them."

Bones sat cracking his knuckles till I'd finished, and most of his belligerence drained away. "You're dead wrong, Son," he told me. "I haven't foreclosed on a single one of 'em."

"I believe you," I said, "but the only reason you haven't is because you couldn't find anyone who would take the junk off your hands—and you haven't found one yet. If you'd come right out in the beginning and told me where you stood, instead of giving me all that blarney about haggling for me, I might have done business with you, but now . . ."

"Now wait a minute, wait a minute, Son," he broke in, this time persuasively instead of irritably. "Don't forget that I wrote all those letters of recommendation for you, and that you're going to make a heap of money on the hauling jobs I got for you. I scratched your back for you when you needed it, now you owe it to me to scratch mine."

"The scratching was fine," I said, "and I appreciate it, but keep your fingernails short; I don't like to be gouged. Now that we're out in the open, maybe we can do some business. I'll gamble time enough to go around and look at the stuff you've marked on the map, and I'll put my bid figure beside each of your offer prices. If we can come to an agreement on the difference, I'll do business with you; if not, I'll buy what I need elsewhere."

The first ten days of August were about as hectic as any I can remember; not because Bones was still trying to hook me—he'd given up on that—but because everything, including the weather, was setting me too fast a pace. Every mail brought more orders for hauling wheat, until I had so many I couldn't have handled them all with a hundred horses. The only honest thing I could do was to write back to some of the owners, telling them I was unable to handle their jobs but would try to find them haulers who could. The big question to decide was which orders to confirm, and which to turn down, and I couldn't do that until I knew when the thrashing would be done on each place. Otherwise, I might have ten times as much hauling as I could handle on some days, and none on others.

Then too, I had to find the horses, harness, and wagons to do the job with, and I had to get them in a hurry, or Gus and Lars wouldn't have time to do the rebuilding. On top of all that, the weather conspired against us. It rained all day on the Saturday after we finished harvesting, turning the roads into a mass of sticky gumbo, and making it necessary to cultivate Mrs. Hudson's corn while we were trying to get ready for the hauling jobs.

Saturday and Sunday would have been lost days if Gus and Lars hadn't moved their repairing into the barn before the old wagons became too wet to work on, and if Kitten hadn't been a cracking good mud horse. I saddled her right after breakfast, turned the other horses out to pasture, put Doc's overalls and jumper on over my own, and started off on the route Bones had drawn on his map.

None of the horses that were offered to me that day were worth their feed, but I found some pretty good harness, a saddle that Paco could use, and a few wagons that could be rebuilt and put into good condition. Whenever I found anything I could use, I marked the price I'd offer for it down beside the price Bones had put on the map, but I kept mine as much below the real value as he had set his above it. It was after dark before I got home, and from being soaked all day my legs had rubbed raw against the saddle, but I'd had better luck than I'd expected. I'd covered more than half the route, found four good sets of harness, five usable wagons, and two double-row cultivators that I rented for a dollar a day until we'd finished with the corn.

Paco and Jaikus had moved our beds into the barn, but the roof leaked more or less, so we spent the whole evening in the kitchen, and I started Judy off on her bookkeeping. Of course, we didn't have any books like those that are used in banks and businesses, but she'd brought a school notebook from home, and it had plenty of room in it for all the accounts we needed to keep track of. Before the war, I'd taken a correspondence course in bookkeeping, and knew there had to be a debit for every credit, but I couldn't remember just how it worked, so we had a few debits without any credits, and a few credits without any debits, but when we finally had our book brought up to date it showed where everybody stood. There was a page for each one in the crew, credited with $256, and charged with whatever he'd drawn: Doc $50, Jaikus $10, and Bill $5. Then I remembered about promising Gus and Lars my first day's pay if they'd stay on the job and double up for Edgar and Everett, so we credited each of them with an extra $4.50.

After we'd finished all the bookkeeping I showed Judy how to make a Profit and Loss Statement for the harvesting. Her handwriting was fine, and it looked like a real business statement, but the profit wasn't as much as I'd hoped it would be, and I owed almost as much as I had in the bank. The statement showed:

Total Income from Harvesting				$2,560.00
Labor	for	"	$1,801.00	
Grub	"	"	148.60	
Repair Parts for	"	"	84.25	
Horses & Eqpt "	"		300.00	
Total Cost of	"			2,333.85
Net Profit from	"			$226.15

Even at that, it wasn't too bad, considering that I had the horses and equipment left.

Sunday morning was bright and clear, but the roads were still too muddy for automobile driving. Right after breakfast I gave Judy all the hauling orders that had come in, and the township maps the County Clerk had marked for me. I told her she'd better figure out some routes, because, as soon as the roads dried, I wanted her to call at each place where I'd heard from the owner, so as to find out the tenant's thrashing dates. Then I set the rest of the crew to helping Gus and Lars, saddled Kitten, and started out to find the rest of the wagons and harness I needed, and to see what might be done about worthwhile horses.

By noon I'd found all the harness and wagons I needed, and had been shown a couple of dozen horses I could have bought for fifty dollars apiece, but there wasn't one of them as good as my old bay mares. I didn't want to stick my neck out and go into debt any deeper than I had to, but I made up my mind that I'd buy the best horses I could find for the job, and pay whatever was necessary to get them.

From then on I had better luck. I headed straight down Beaver Valley, stopped only at the most prosperous looking places, and told the men who came out to meet me exactly what I was looking for—small, young, mustang horses, that had been worked enough through the spring and summer to be hard and tough. I told them that I didn't care how ornery or hard to handle they might be, as long as they had plenty of go and toughness. The farmers I called on didn't have that kind of horses, but sent me on to places where they thought I might find them. I didn't have time to get around to all the places, but by sunset I'd bought four cracking good teams—and they'd cost me $885. What's more, I'd made friends with a lot of prosperous farmers, and found that I could hire all the teams of heavy horses I wanted, together with first-rate wagons, for five dollars a day.

By Monday the roads had dried enough that I could drive the Maxwell, so I strated out with it as soon as we'd had breakfast. I stopped only at the places where I'd been told I might find the kind of horses I wanted, let the farmer set his price on any team I'd have been glad to own, then drove on to the next place. By the time I'd finished my round, I'd seen eight or ten teams that were just what I needed, and the prices ranged anywhere from $200 to $250 a team. I set my limit at $200, then started back to make the round again, but made my bid only on the best teams. I failed to get the two that I liked best, but by half-past-nine I'd bought the next best three.

I was waiting outside the bank when Bones unlocked the door that morning. He acted grouchy when I told him I was going to buy no horses from farmers he'd sent me to, and he screamed like a trapped wildcat when I showed him the prices I was offering on the wagons and harness. I spent an hour haggling with him, just to let him feel he'd made the best deal he was going to get, then told him, "I'll tell you what 'll do: you add up all the figures you put down on the map for these items, then add up my offers, and I'll split the difference with you. If that doesn't suit you, I'll have to take a drive over to Oberlin."

I think Bones had known where we'd end up as well as I had, but a deal of that kind isn't a good one without a little haggling, and we'd both had fun doing it. Of course, we told each other we'd been stuck by a sharper trader, but we were both tickled enough to squirm with our ends of the bargain. I'd bought equipment for $720 that I'd thought would cost me nearly $1000, and he'd collected $720 on loans that he'd believed to be dead losses.

Mrs. Hudson fixed us an early dinner, and by noon we had the old Maxwell back on the road, loaded with the whole crew, and Judy doing the driving. First we picked up the horses, then went on at a pace no faster than they could trot comfortably, until we'd picked up all the harness and wagons. As soon as we had a set of harness and a wagon together, we dropped off a driver and pair of horses, then drew a map so he'd know where to pick up another wagon or a cultivator on the way home. It was mid-afternoon when Judy dropped me off, then went on to make some of her calls. I hadn't driven more than a mile before I knew that the horses I was holding the reins on were exactly the kind I needed. Even though they'd been at an almost steady trot for four hours, they were as full of go as if they'd been fresh from the corral—and I let them go.

Being the last one dropped, I was last to get back to the place, and anyone might have thought there was a barn raising going on there. Eight wagons were drawn up in the yard, the harness spread over the wheels, and the corral was a heaving mass of tough little broncos. They were biting, kicking, and laying their ears back as they got acquainted with each other, but it was easy to see that they'd discovered who the boss was; Kitten was feeding by herself, and the new horses were all giving her a wide berth. I pulled my wagon in beside the others, and Paco helped me unharness. Then we wasted an hour, standing by the corral gate and gloating over the horses. I was the proudest I'd ever been in my life, but I was in debt $2000, and the only part of my bank account that belonged to me was $16.15. When I mentioned it there wasn't a man in the crew who didn't tell me to use his share of the account as though it had been my own.

12

Tricky Business

I don't believe I slept more than an hour the night we brought the new horses home, but lay awake, thinking and planning. The success or failure of my new business wouldn't depend alone on tough, fast horses, but on using wagons in pairs, and that was going to be tricky business. There were sharp corners to turn, steep hills to go down as well as up, and the elevator rocker to be coped with. The rocker was a great trap door in the floor of a narrow driveway through the elevator. When a wagon was pulled onto it, the wheels were blocked, the endgate removed, and the rocker tilted to dump the load into the grain pit below.

With light horses and trailers, the uphill climbs would be rugged, but it was the steep downgrades that worried me. A wagon and trailer, each loaded with fifty bushels of wheat, would weigh about four tons, and two light horses on the pole couldn't possibly keep it from running wild. Both wagon and trailer would have to be held back by over-sized brakes, and a driver could actuate them only if the trailer were coupled close and rigidly to the lead wagon. Still, the coupling would have to be flexible enough to allow for sharp turns, and to permit each wagon to be tilted separately on the elevator rocker.

Ever since I'd first had the idea of hauling with trailers, I'd been trying to figure out types of coupling and brake rigs that would do the job the way it would have to be done. Some of those I'd thought of were so complicated that I could hardly keep track of all the pieces in my mind, but as I lay there in the darkness I suddenly had an idea, so simple that any child might have thought of it. All I had to do was to have heavy angle irons bent into the shape of three-foot V's, with hinges at the upper ends, and the point flattened out to make a turnplate with a bolt hole at the center.

By hinging one V to the back axle of the lead wagon, and another on the front axle of the trailer, the coupling would be made when the two turnplates were bolted together. It would hold one wagon rigidly behind the other, with no possibility of swaying, but the pivot bolt would make it possible to turn sharp corners, and the hinges would allow each wagon to be tilted separately on the elevator rocker. Then, too, that type of coupling solved my brake problem, as the pivot bolt would give me a dead center between the front and back wagon. By using an eyebolt, I could run a steel cable through the eye, connecting the brake beam on the trailer with a foot pedal on the lead wagon, and the pressure could be held constant, no matter how sharp a downhill curve might be.

Tuesday morning we loaded the cultivators onto our best wagon, harnessed six of the new horses, and I sent Old Bill, Jaikus, and Paco to begin the corn cultivating. Judy drove ahead to show them were the quarter-section was, then would go on from there to make more calls on tenants, so as to list their thrashing schedules.

As soon as they had driven away I called Gus, Lars, and Doc to the middle of the yard. There I drew on a ground a full-sized plan of the coupling and brake assembly I'd thought of during the night, and asked them if they could see any reason it wouldn't work, or could think of anything that might be better. Doc made up his mind within two minutes, but Gus and Lars studied the plan for at least fifteen minutes, mumbling to each other in Swedish, before they told me they thought it would be the best we could do.

Next, we went over each wagon carefully, listing the parts and lumber we'd need for each one, since the repairing would be our biggest job in getting ready for the hauling. Every wheel had to be taken apart, new spokes and fellies shaped and fitted into place where the old ones were cracked or broken, and the tires sweated back on so tightly there would be no possibility of their loosening or slipping under the most severe use. Weak tongues, stretchers, bolsters, axles, and doubletrees had to be replaced. The bodies had to be rebuilt and strengthened with steel bands, making them almost water-tight, so they wouldn't leak wheat when jounced over rough roads. New side boards had to be fitted in here and there, new front-gates and end-gates made, seats repaired, and over-sized brakes made and installed, together with seven sets of coupling rigs.

It was mid-forenoon when we finished examining the wagons and making up lists of the tools and materials we'd need for the job, so I said, "Let's harness a team and drive to Oberlin. There's a lot of this stuff we couldn't get at The Bluffs, and I want to start a blacksmith working on those coupling irons right away."

As I spoke, I picked up a set of harness from a wagon wheel and started toward the corral. I expected the others to follow me, but they didn't. When I looked back from the corral gate, Gus and Lars were still standing where I'd left them, and they appeared to be arguing, but Doc was nowhere in sight.

Alone, and without a throw rope, I had a little trouble in catching the pair of horses I wanted. It might have taken me fifteen minutes to catch and harness them, and when I led them to one of the wagons Gus and Lars were waiting for me. Gus did the talking, and I couldn't have been more surprised if I'd discovered that Doc was actually an M.D. They were blacksmiths by trade, but had sold their shop in the spring, and had planned to spend the summer seeing the country, then go

on to California for the winter. They'd intended to put in only
a week at harvesting, just long enough to see how it was done
in the West.

What they'd been arguing about was whether it would be
cheaper for me to buy an anvil, iron working tools, and bricks
and bellows for a forge, or to have our work done by a blacksmith
in town. There was no question in my mind. Half the job of rebuilding the wagons would be iron work and resetting the tires.
Doc and I could do the woodwork, and if they could do our
blacksmithing right on the place it would save us several days
time, so the cost didn't matter too much.

With angle iron, materials for a forge, and lumber to haul,
we'd have too heavy a load for two light horses, so I told Gus,
"We'll use a four-horse hitch. If you'll rig a doubletree to the
end of that wagon pole, I'll get the long reins and have another
team ready in a few minutes."

I was so excited about being able to do our own blacksmithing right on the place that I'd forgotten there was any such a
man as Doc, but he didn't let me forget it long. As I hurried into
the barn for the reins, his vibrant medicine-man oratory came
rolling toward me like a tidal wave from the darkness of the
farthest stall, "My dear companion, some treacherous oaf has
sullied my raiment with foul and offensive offal, and to escape
detection of his perfidious act has ensconced it . . ."

"Hold it, Doc! Save it till we get to town," I called back. "We're
both treacherous oafs; you did the sullying when you got into
the tanglefoot, and I did the ensconcing when I shucked the
raiment off you."

As my eyes became accustomed to the dimness, I could see
Doc standing at the end of the farthest stall, dressed in his
wrinkled and dirty medicine-man clothes, and trying to wipe
some of the grime off his frock coat with his work shirt. "Better
get out of those fancy duds, and back into your overalls," I
told him. "We've got a lot of work to do in town, and you can
have that gorgeous raiment cleaned and pressed while we're
doing it."

By the time I'd caught and harnessed the second team, Doc was not only back in his overalls, but back to being a harvest hand. He'd stowed his raiment, carefully wrapped in news-paper, in the wagon, and he'd stowed his oratory right along with it.

I knew that a lot of men found a tremendous thrill in getting behind the wheel of an automobile and tramping the gas pedal clear to the floor, but it didn't do very much for me. Maybe it was because horses were too much in my blood, but I found a lot more fun in sitting on the high seat of a jouncing wagon, and shaking the lines above the backs of a fast-stepping four-horse hitch—particularly if the horses were my own. In choos-ing the horses for cultivating, I'd tried to pick out the steadiest teams in the new bunch, but for the trip to town I'd picked the four toughest and liveliest—and they didn't disappoint me.

Doc held the bridles of the snap team until I was on the seat with the lines gathered between my fingers, and Gus and Lars were standing with a good hold on the back of the seat. Then Doc turned the little broncs loose, scrambled up onto the seat beside me, and we were on our way in a cloud of dust. As we swung out of the yard with the wheels skidding, anyone might have thought I was an old-time stage driver, trying to escape the Comanches. I could almost have believed it myself. The teams had come from different places, and each seemed to be trying to outrun the other. The wagon we'd hitched to was in pretty good shape and we had a straight, level half mile to the first corner, so I let the horses work off a little of their fire. I cocked one foot up on the brake pedal, shook the lines enough to keep the bit rings jingling, and shouted, "Hya! Haa! Haa!"

We covered that half mile like Man o' War coming down the home stretch. As we neared the corner, I braced myself against the brake pedal till the hind wheels squealed like fighting hogs, leaned back on the seat, and gathered the reins to make a stab at keeping in the roadway as we made the turn. We made it, with the wagon slewing around as though it had been on slick ice, but it wasn't because of my skill with the reins. That little snap team knew its business so much better than I knew mine that it made me feel silly. They didn't turn the instant they reached the corner, but kept straight on for another length, giving the wagon room to clear the turn, then swung over so fast they were leaning at a 45° angle, and neither horse ever missed a beat in his stride. I was too busy watching the snap team to pay any attention to the wheelers, but they must have had to lean fully as far, and I don't believe they ever left the wheel tracks.

I let them have another Hya! Haa! Haa! as soon as we'd rounded the corner, and while Doc, Gus, and Lars clung to the seat with both hands, the old wagon went leaping along the roadway like a frightened jack rabbit. After a quarter mile I soft-talked the broncs down to a spanking trot, then let them hold it till we reached the county road, a mile and a quarter farther on.

We followed the county road ten miles into Oberlin, and by the time we got there I wouldn't have sold that four-horse hitch for twice what I'd paid for it—and on the way I learned a few things that were going to help us in our hauling business. Where the road was fairly level I held the team to a moderate trot, then when we came to a gulch I let them take off at a dead run, giving the wagon just enough brake that it wouldn't run up onto the wheelers' heels. Just before we swooped through the bottom of each gulch, I kicked the brake loose, giving the wagon its full momentum to race up the hill beyond. A man would be out of his mind to run most horses downhill the way I ran those little cayuses, but they had so much mustang in them that they were sure-footed as mountain goats, and I knew there wasn't the slightest danger that any one of them would stumble and fall. Of course, if one had, the next passer-by might have had to pick us up in pieces.

That trip to town took us no more than an hour, and when we reached the main street my snap team was still fresh enough to rear and spook at noisy jalopies. They kept me plenty busy until we'd pulled off the main street and into the yard of a blacksmith's shop. Gus and Lars thought it would be best to stop there first, so they could find out from the blacksmith whether or not there was a supplier in Oberlin who carried steel, and the blacksmithing tools and equipment they would need. As soon as they'd gone inside, Doc fished his bundle out from under the seat, and told me, "I'd better take this stuff over to the tailor's shop right away, so they'll have time to get it cleaned and pressed while we're picking up our load. Write me a check for twenty, will you?"

I was in a bit of a spot. Doc had a couple of hundred dollars coming to him, so I couldn't refuse to write him a check for any part of it he asked for, but I didn't feel too safe about him. As I pulled out my checkbook, I said, "Sure, Doc, you can draw whatever you want, but don't you get into the tanglefoot again. If Gus and Lars do the blacksmithing, I'll need your help with the woodwork, and you won't be any help if you're plastered."

"Aw, Bud," he said in an injured tone, "you know me better'n that. You know I wouldn't let you down at a time like this! Just because I stubbed my toe once, you don't have to rub it in with a rough cob. If you can't spare twenty, five'll do. Only thing is, I'd like to pick up a couple of pairs of overalls and some shirts before we go back."

"Sorry, Doc," I told him as I wrote the check for twenty dollars, "I wasn't rubbing it in, and I know you're the last man in the crew that would let me down. Maybe I'm too jumpy about this hauling business and getting the wagons fixed up. I didn't sleep worth a dime last night."

"Don't lose any sleep over me and the corn squeezings," he told me as he climbed down over the wheel. "Only time I have any trouble with the stuff is when I get one of my seizures, and I don't get more than two or three of 'em in a year's time. You wait right here for me; I'll be back in ten minutes."

Doc wasn't back in ten minutes, or twenty, and neither were Gus and Lars. I could see them inside the shop, talking with the blacksmith, walking all around the place, and looking it over as though they might be planning to buy it. And the longer they looked the more jumpy my nerves got. If I lost those two men, and Doc went on a bender, my hauling business would be blown sky high.

By the time another ten minutes had passed I was so keyed up that I could have flown—and with no more than two feathers on each shoulder blade. When I was almost ready to explode, Gus and Lars came out to the wagon, bringing the blacksmith with them. He was fully as big as they, and as slow spoken. He spit a stream of tobacco juice at the near wheeler's heels, cocked a foot in the hub, and said, "Your men tell me you aim to set up a shop, but there ain't a supplier no nearer than Denver, and it would take leastways a fortnight to get a shipment out. We been lookin' around my shop, and I reckon I could spare enough tools to get you by, along with an anvil and an old bellows that could be patched up, but I'd have to charge you twenty-five dollars for the use of 'em. I got plenty of strap steel and angle iron on hand, but I'd have to have cash on the barrel head— you being a stranger hereabouts."

I had my checkbook out before he'd mentioned the barrel head. "Will a check do it?" I asked him. "You can call the banker over at Cedar Bluffs to find out whether or not it's any good."

"No need of that," he told me, "and no sense writing a check till we figure up what your steel will come to. From what your men tell me, it'll prob'ly run up to fifty, sixty dollars."

There was no doubt in my mind that Doc had been taken with another seizure, but by that time I didn't care how much of a bender he went on; I was too happy about not having lost Gus and Lars, and that we were going to be able to set up a shop for almost nothing. "Come on," I told them. "Let's leave the team here and go get some dinner. There's no sense in waiting any longer for Doc; he's probably holed up in some speakeasy. We can talk about what we'll do next while we're eating." We decided that it would be best for Lars to stay at the blacksmith's shop, to pick out the tools, equipment, and steel, while Gus and I bought the rest of the stuff we would need.

If I'd been alone, I'd have gone into the office at the lumber-yard, said I wanted top-grade hickory or white oak, given my order for the number of pieces and sizes, then let the yardman get me out the nearest he had to it. Gus didn't go at it that way. He insisted on going into the yard himself, examining the entire stock of hardwood, picking out heavy timbers with straight, flawless grain, then having the millwright saw and plane them into the exact sizes we needed. At the hardware store he was as slow and careful in choosing every tool, bolt, or other item. Most of my time was taken in finding Manila line for catch ropes, extender reins, collars for the new horses, and harness-mending supplies. It was late afternoon before we'd loaded the bricks, sand, cement, and coal for the forge.

During the afternoon I'd thought of Doc a dozen times, but had pushed him out of my mind, thinking we'd find him asleep in the pool hall when we were ready to go home. That wasn't where we found him. On our way back to the blacksmith's shop we were driving past the stockyards when, from among the cattle pens, I heard Doc's voice, "Gen'lmen, I have a purpose." There was enough slur to the words that it left no doubt as to what his purpose had been, or that he'd accomplished it. I pulled the team up, passed Gus the reins, and said, "I guess I'd better go and collect Doc while we know where he is."

There were a dozen or so men, hooting and laughing, at the far end of the yards, and Doc, rigged out in his medicine-man raiment, towered above their heads. Twice, as I hurried toward the group, Doc tried to make his pitch again, but both times he stalled on the "purpose," and had to start over. I'd reached the edge of the crowd before I discovered what all the hooting was about. Doc was perched like a crowing rooster on the end of a long plank watering trough, and each time he filled his lungs to orate he lost his balance long enough that he had to regain it by flapping his arms as though they'd been wings.

"Doc!" I shouted to him. "Come on, we're heading out!"

I have an idea that Doc's sight was blurred enough to see a multitude, and that he couldn't recognize me in the throng.

Although everyone else looked my way, Doc didn't but launched into his oration again. Sometimes a fellow gets ideas faster than he has time to reason them out, and a few flashed through my head when I couldn't catch Doc's attention. One was that he'd get polluted every time he dressed up and came to town. Another was that he might keep sober if he didn't have his fancy clothes, or if they could be so completely ruined that he couldn't wear them. And the third was that a good dousing in cold water might sober him enough that I could get him back to the wagon.

It all went through my head so fast that the crowd was still looking my way when I got the dousing idea. I winked at a young farm hand who was standing by the trough, and made a motion as though I were pulling a handkerchief out of my hip pocket. The boy winked back, then gave Doc's coat tail a quick jerk. He went over backwards faster than Kitten had gone over with me.

Water splashed ten feet high, and Doc came up blowing like a whale. I got there just in time to help him out over the edge of the trough, and the shock had sobered him enough to recognize me. "My dear companion," he burbled, "some foul fiend has . . ." Then he had a spasm of coughing and blowing water.

I gave him a couple of slaps on the back, locked an arm under mine, and told him, "Let's get out of here before another fiend gets you. For a bone-dry town, this one seems to be full of them." Reeling, hiccupping, and shedding water like a sprinkler wagon, Doc let me lead him to the wagon, where Gus helped me lift him aboard and lay him out on a bed of bricks.

Lars had everything we needed laid out and ready for loading when we got back to the blacksmith's shop, but Doc had given up the battle. He was snoring like a contented sow, and slept right through our hoisting him to the top of the lumber pile, so as to make room for the steel and blacksmithing equipment. The wagon was heaped high when we pulled out of town—and I was $223 deeper in debt.

As near as we could figure, our load weighed about three and

a half tons, or as much as a hundred and twenty bushels of wheat, and there was a rise of several hundred feet from Oberlin to the Hudson place. It gave me a good chance to find out what lightweight horses could do with a heavy load on hilly roads, and I was more than pleased with what I learned. Where an upgrade was long and gradual, my horses had to pull with all their might, and I had to rest them often. On level ground they handled the pull easily, trotted right along on the downgrades, and swooped through the gulches like swallows. The thrust of the heavy load on the downhill run into a gulch was enough to carry the wagon well up the far side. Then my little mustangs drove into their collars with everything they had, scrambling to the top before the momentum was entirely lost. With a two-minute breather there, they were ready to do it all over again. Even with the heavy load and the rise, we covered the twelve miles home in a little over two and a half hours.

Gus and Lars unloaded Doc while I unharnessed, then we peeled off his soaking raiment, rolled him in a blanket, and left him to sleep off his seizure. Coal and cement dust had settled like soot when we'd loaded the wagon, and Doc's wet raiment had absorbed it as a blotter will absorb ink. Before we went in to supper I piled the soggy heap against the east side of the barn, where the morning sun would dry it into a fair imitation of granite.

After supper Judy and I sat at the kitchen table, trying to fit together a jigsaw puzzle, while the rest of the crew unloaded the wagon. Our puzzle wasn't really made up of pieces cut with a jigsaw, but was even more complicated, because we had a lot more pieces than we knew what to do with, and they wouldn't fit together worth a cent.

Judy had called at all the places from which I'd received hauling orders by Saturday, but the mailman had brought seven more since then, and there were still five days till August 10th—the date I'd set as a dead line in my letters. Worse still, the orders were scattered over an area of a hundred square miles, and some of the tenants hadn't yet set their thrashing dates, while others had arranged for the same weeks, extending into early October. If we'd started working on our puzzle the evening before, I'd have separated out for refusal all orders where thrashing would begin before August 29th, for Mrs. Hudson's hauling was expected to take eighteen days, beginning on the 11th, and I'd planned to buy barely enough horses and wagons to keep up with the thrasher.

All my figuring had been done on the hope that each four-horse rig could haul a hundred bushels of wheat twenty miles in a day. I'd reasoned that since the distance from the Hudson place to the elevator was eight miles, each rig could make two and a half trips, and that my six rigs could haul a maximum of 1500 bushels a day. I'd changed my mind while we'd been bringing the load home from Oberlin.

That trip with a heavy load had taught me that it was the lay of the land which would determine how many bushels of wheat I could haul in a day. If all my horses could swoop through gulches as the little team I'd been driving did, I'd only have to change my plans slightly in order to haul 120 bushels on each trip instead of 100. All that would be necessary was to put my tote teams at the long upgrades rather than at the deep gulches. If that would work, I'd be able to haul 1800 bushels eight miles in a day, and Mrs. Hudson's job would require only 1400. At the same time I was doing her work I'd be able to haul 400 bushels the same distance for some other customer, or 800 bushels half that distance. The problem was to pick out jobs where the output of the thrashing machine and the distance to the elevator would match the hauling I could handle.

Beyond that, if I could find enough hauling over roads that were ideally suited to my kind of horses, there was no doubt in my mind that I could stretch the distance of my hauls by a mile or two. But I'd be in trouble if I took any jobs that wouldn't work out to full round-trips, for I'd have to keep part of my horses and men at the wrong end of the line. With the number of widely scattered orders I already had, and from what I'd learned about the surrounding country while hunting for horses and equipment, I believed the problem could be solved.

Beaver Creek snaked its way from southwest to northeast where it crossed the line from Kansas into Nebraska. The valley floor was flat, and little more than a half mile wide, with the railroad skirting the foot of the hills that fringed the high, gulch-torn divide to the south, while the land to the north rose more gently. Cedar Bluffs was the last Kansas town on the railroad, with Marion, Nebraska seven miles below. Most of the hauling orders I'd received were for delivery to the elevator in one of those towns; some from up or down the valley, some from the gently sloping country to the north, and others from the rugged, high divide to the south.

The first thing Judy and I did was to weed out all the orders which required long hauls along the level valley floor. The roads there would become gummy if we had any rain, and it seemed better to let that business go to haulers with heavier, slower horses. Then we began matching orders where the big 1400-bushel-a-day thrashing rigs were going to be used. Unless the distances to the elevator averaged no more than five miles, there would be no sense in trying to keep up with two of such machines at the same time. Of course, I could do it by hiring enough extra horses, wagons, and drivers, but it seemed best to let someone else have one of the jobs. All we needed to decide was which one to keep.

Next we laid aside all the orders from the north side of the valley. The rises and falls were in much longer sweeps than on the high divide, and my little horses wouldn't be too good on those long uphill pulls. Then too, if I took jobs that far from the Hudson place, I'd wear my horses down too much in coming and going. That left us with fewer pieces for our puzzle, but still with too many, and at first it looked as though none of them would fit together. The distances from the ranches to the elevators ranged from three to thirteen miles, and the output of the machines from eight to fourteen hundred bushels a day. On top of that, I couldn't estimate how many bushels a day we could haul from any one of those places until I knew every detail of the road between it and the elevator to which we'd be hauling. I'd have to ask Judy, "How many miles is it from that Wickham quarter to The Bluffs, and how big is the thrashing rig the tenant is going to use?"

After she'd counted them off on the township maps, she'd tell me, "Well, it's ten and a half miles to the school house, so you might as leave call it eleven to the elevator, and Hunsinger is going to do the thrashing, so that will be about twelve hundred bushels a day—if he don't have no breakdowns, but he generally always does; his rig's kind of an old one."

"Now try to remember," I'd say, "how many hills will we have to pull that are as long and steep as that one just south of the buildings on the Moss place?"

While Judy chewed the end of her pencil, she'd mumble around it, "Well, there's that one by Wes Ridgeway's place, and that one by Blickenstaff's . . no, you got three by Blickenstaff's; one before you turn the corner, and then two after."

"Never mind," I'd tell her, as I laid the order for the Wickham quarter section aside. "Suppose you take a look at the mileage from the De May place to The Bluffs."

By eleven o'clock we had no two pieces of the puzzle fitted together, but we did know the pieces that we weren't going to use, and we'd found some others that came fairly close to fitting. There was no use in trying to go any further until we'd had a chance to drive the old Maxwell over every foot of the routes we'd have to travel for each job, so I could look the hills over carefully, and figure out which jobs would work best for my type of horses.

I expected the crew to have turned in as soon as they had the wagon unloaded, but when I left the kitchen I could see a torch burning near the corner of the barn, and another speck of light that I knew would be from the lantern. Until my eyes became a bit used to the darkness, I couldn't see the men, but they were all there—all but Doc. Paco was sitting with the old bellows in his lap, patching the cracked leather with pieces of rawhide, stuck tight with beeswax, and sewn securely with rawhide thongs. Old Bill and Jaikus were being hod carriers for Gus and Lars, who had already laid most of the bricks for their forge. All that was left to do was to set in the draft duct, attach the bellows, and lay the two top courses of bricks. About all the help I could be was in holding the torch where it would give them the best light until they were finished—just before one o'clock.

13

Wagon Wheels

WHEN we'd stripped Doc of his ruined finery we'd put his arms at his sides, rolled him in a blanket, and laid him out on a bed of straw as though he were a mummy. The next morning he was exactly as we'd left him, his mouth still open, and snoring like a geyser on the verge of erupting. I had two reasons for leaving him right there when we went to breakfast. In the first place, he wouldn't be worth a nickel until his hangover had worn off, and in the second, I wanted the sun to have plenty of time to dry his wadded raiment and harden the cement in it.

As we left our camp we stopped to look at the little forge Gus and Lars had built, and I could see that the other fellows were much more interested in the work that would be going on at the place than in cultivating corn, but it was as necessary as any of our other jobs. I'd planned that, with three teams in the field, the job would take four days, but to let the men know they weren't being pushed aside, I said, "I sure hate to spare you fellows at a time like this. Would it help to hurry the job along if you took three extra teams this morning, so you could change horses at noon?"

"Sure would," Old Bill told me. "If we could trade teams at

noon, and if the missus would put us up some dinner, so's't we didn't have to come back here to eat, we could wind that job up by tomorrow night."

In the month we'd been together Paco had picked up maybe a hundred words of English, but he'd learned them all from Jaikus, so they had an amusing Irish twist to them, and he never used them with me. As we walked toward the windmill to wash for breakfast I told him in Spanish what I'd told Old Bill and Jaikus. I didn't intend for my talk to set a fire under them, but they acted as if it had. They stuffed away ham, eggs, and flap-jacks to beat the band, while Mrs. Hudson packed a milk bucket with dinner for them. Paco left the table with half his break-fast in his hand, and even Gus and Lars seemed to have caught the fever.

I stopped to tell Judy that, as soon as she'd made her calls about the new orders, I wanted her to look for haulers who might like to take the jobs we were going to turn down. Then I wrote a list of the farmers who had offered to rent me teams, and said they'd probably be the best ones to start off with. I couldn't have spent more than ten minutes with her, but just as I left the kitchen the cultivator crew pulled out of the yard at a spanking trot, leading six spare horses behind the wagon.

Gus and Lars were at the barn, cribbing up sections of old wagon tongues to make a base for their anvil, and I went to help them with it. I knew only enough about blacksmithing to shoe a horse or weld a point onto a plowshare, but woodworking was no novelty to me, and though I didn't know much about wagon building, Gus and Lars would show me the new tricks I'd have to learn.

We spent our first couple of hours building work benches along the front of the barn, putting up shelves for our tools and hardware, and in sorting out our various sizes and shapes of steel and lumber. Then we started tearing the old wagons down; lifting off the bodies, removing the wheels, cold-chiseling rusted bolts out of bolsters and axles, and building a bonfire to burn the steel fittings off cracked or broken singletrees, neck yokes, seats, end-gates, and wagon tongues.

Chopping bolts with cold-chisels doesn't produce lullaby music, but Doc slept through it until nearly noon. Then he came shuffling from behind the barn, back in his overalls, and with his face so swollen it looked as if he'd been in the poison ivy. I caught a glimpse of him as he came around the corner, but kept right on with the bolt I was chopping, and didn't look up again. He came over to the wagon I was working on, and I could see by his shadow that he was standing there dejectedly. He waited until the head snapped off the bolt, then mumbled, "I'm sorry, Bud. I didn't aim to let you down like . . ."

"You didn't let me down; I let you down—into the watering trough," I told him. "It was the only way I could think of to get you home, and I couldn't risk losing you at a time like this. There's nothing for you to be sorry about, unless it's that hangover, and if ever a man earned a blowout, you have. I couldn't have lasted a week at that stacking job. Get yourself a bellyful of cold milk, and take it easy for the rest of the day, then you and I will light into this carpentry work tomorrow."

Doc had been standing, head down, and facing toward the barn. When I'd finished, he looked up at me, came as close to grinning as he could with a hangover such as his, and said, "You can count on me from here out, Bud. Looks like you did a right good job of getting me out of the medicine-show business. Knew all along that you'd never go into it with me."

Before I could think of anything to say, Doc walked to the heap of almost rock-hard clothes that lay at the end of my bench, picked it up, and tossed it into the center of the bonfire. During the afternoon he worked as hard as any one of us, but I'll bet it was one of the toughest afternoons he ever put in.

It was after sunset before either Judy or the cultivating crew came back, and by that time we had every piece of cracked, worn, or broken lumber out of the old wagons, the fittings burned away, the old rivets and bolts chopped out, and were ready to begin the rebuilding the first thing next morning. Judy had found seven or eight men who were glad to take on part of the hauling work we were going to turn down, and Old Bill said the corn field was already two-thirds finished.

That night the crew turned in early, but Judy and I sat up until after midnight, driving the roads, and working on our puzzle. We started by driving very slowly over the road from the Hudson place to the elevator in Cedar Bluffs. There was a steep little rise to pull just after leaving the place, then two long upgrades farther on; one of them three miles from the ranch, and the other three miles out from town. Except for the two deep gulches, the rest of the way was mostly downgrade, with the last mile quite steep.

Right from the beginning I'd planned to use my old mares as an extra team for pulling wagons out of the fields. By leaving them hitched on for another half mile, the sharp little rise would be no trouble to us. Then I could put a hired tote team at the foot of each of the two long upgrades. I wouldn't need drivers for them, but would keep feed at the foot of the rise, so the horses would return after each pull. With help up those long grades, and with the rest of the way mostly downhill, my only big worry was the gulches. If all my teams could swoop through them at an all-out run, we could easily haul 120-bushel loads, and I'd be able to handle a smaller job along with the Hudson hauling. By running the gulches, my fast horses could easily haul a load to town in two hours, and return with the empty wagons in even less time. But if I had to use tote teams there, I'd lose a half hour at each gulch, so it wouldn't do me any good to haul an extra twenty bushels at each trip. My teams couldn't get over the road fast enough to keep up with more than one thrashing rig.

Every man I had would be glad to work a twelve-hour day, but the horses, tough as I knew them to be, couldn't do it on that kind of work. I was pretty sure they could travel forty-two to forty-four miles a day, half with a load and half without, but I'd risk breaking them down if I tried to stretch it.

Even if my horses could run the gulches, I didn't want to take an additional job where we'd have to haul more than 800 bushels a day, and only five miles instead of eight. Then too, it would have to be over the last five miles of the route we'd be using for the Hudson job, so as to use the same tote team on the last upgrade. There wasn't any such job among the orders I'd received, but there were six—for quarter-sections, and two halves—that would fit in fairly well. They were all between the Hudson place and Cedar Bluffs, the dates matched up all right, and the thrashing was going to be done by two fairly small rigs. There were only two big difficulties; the distances averaged nearly six miles instead of five, and one of the machines was rated to thrash a thousand bushels a day, the other eight hundred.

I didn't like to take an unreasonable risk, but decided to take all those jobs. It didn't seem probable that all three thrashing rigs would operate at full capacity every hour of every day. There would surely be a few breakdowns, and the smaller machines would lose time in moving from one place to another. Besides that, I could hire extra wagons and drivers on the days I'd need them, so there wasn't too much danger that I'd fall down on the job for any of my customers.

I'd been lucky enough to get the hauling from the next two jobs to be done by the thrashing rig Mrs. Hudson had engaged. They were both full-section jobs, a few miles farther to the north, and the hauling was to be done to the Marion, Nebraska elevator. It was ten o'clock before we had the first part of our puzzle put together, then I had Judy drive me over the route for the two big jobs.

If I'd had my choice of all the wheat hauling jobs to be done in Kansas, I couldn't have found two that would have been any better suited to my little horses. Both sections were at the very top of the high divide between Beaver and Sappa creeks, and both were within a mile of the county road; one of them seven miles out from the elevator, and the other eight. The first two or three miles were nearly level, then the last five were almost a toboggan slid down to the elevator. There was only one bad stretch of a half mile in the whole distance, and an extra team could easily take care of that.

The second half of our puzzle was just the opposite of the first. Although I still had more orders than I could handle, there weren't enough of them on that high divide, or on the slope between there and Beaver Valley, to keep all my teams busy every day. If I had to fill in with hauling from any other part of the area, I'd only wear my men and horses down, and couldn't hope to make but very little profit from their work.

As soon as Judy had driven me down to have a look at the elevator in Marion, I had her take me back to the house, and there we fitted into our puzzle the smaller orders I'd received for hauling from the high divide. Some of them overlapped enough that there would be days when I'd have to hire five or six extra wagons and drivers. And there were some good sized holes, where I wouldn't have work enough for more than half of my own teams.

By midnight I'd decided that we'd better fill in the schedule with scattered jobs, and we were looking through the orders to see which ones might work out best when Judy said, "You know, Bud, it ain't only owners that live someplace else that let out hauling. Most of them that farm their own places can't handle more'n half their hauling at thrashing time. They have to let the rest of it out, and they pay the same price as the landlords. It's cheaper for 'em to do that than to hire haulers by the day, 'cause a man don't work his horses very hard when he's hiring 'em out by the day. If you'd leave me try, I'll bet I could get us enough fill-in jobs right over there on the divide, or on the way down to Marion. Lots of people don't think nothing about letting out their hauling till thrashing time's right on top of 'em."

I not only liked Judy's idea, but I liked her saying, "get *us* enough fill-in jobs."

"You go after them as hard as you can go," I told her, "and don't pass up any that come in our slack times, no matter how small they are, or even if they're out of rugged back country. We'll put on whatever extra teams we need, and with those short, downhill runs we could handle half the haul from three or four thrashing rigs. Now run along and get yourself some sleep, and don't you start out before nine o'clock tomorrow morning. I can't afford to have you wear yourself down to a nubbin before we ever start the hauling business."

She tried to tell me I was the one who was wearing himself down, and that I was getting skinnier every day, but I knew I wasn't and that the toughest end of the job was already behind me, so I stayed up until I'd written to all the owners whose jobs we couldn't handle, giving each one the names of other haulers who would take their work.

Thursday morning the cultivating crew was away by sunup, Gus and Lars were starting the fire in their forge, and Doc and I were shaving new spokes for wagon wheels. An hour later I heard the old Maxwell backfire, then Judy drove away to begin hunting for fill-in jobs on the high divide.

With only four days left until thrashing time, the wheels worried me more than any part of our job, for the success of my business would depend as much on sturdy wheels as on tough horses. There was hardly one on the wagons I'd bought that didn't need a couple of new spokes or fellies, and a few needed twice that many. Reinforcing bands had to be forged for the weakened hubs, all the tires cut, rewelded to the proper size, expanded by heating, then forced onto the repaired woodwork to bind it in a viselike grip as the metal cooled and shrank —and twelve wagons meant forty-eight wheels.

Once the wheels were out of the way, the rest of the job wouldn't require too much carpentry. Gus had been so careful in selecting the lumber, and so insistent that it be milled to exactly the right sizes, that the stretchers, bolsters, axle beams, side boards, and end-gates would require only sawing and shaping. The tongues and singletrees would need only to be tapered with a drawknife, then smoothed with a spokeshave, and the seats would need only to have the corners rounded. In mounting the metal fittings to the wood there'd be hundreds of holes to be bored, bolts and rivets to be driven through, and nuts and washers to be turned and peened tight, but most of it was work that Old Bill, Jaikus, and Paco could do.

Within an hour we'd settled into a steady routine. Although Doc wasn't a highly skilled carpenter, he had an excellent knack for using tools, his hangover was completely gone, and he seemed anxious to make up for the time he'd lost. With hardly a pause between each one, he'd snatch up a spoke that needed replacing, saw a piece of lumber to exactly the same length, clamp it into his vise, strip it roughly round with a few strokes of a drawknife, and smooth it with a spokeshave. Then, as I cut tenons on the new spoke, he'd rough out a felly for me to mortise and finish.

Doc set so hot a pace that he kept the sweat pouring off the rest of us in order to keep up with him, but we rebuilt wheels a lot faster than I'd have believed we could. Though sweat streamed from them, Gus and Lars never seemed to hurry, but as fast as we had the new spokes and fellies cut and shaped for a wheel, they had the hub bands in place, and a smoking hot tire ready to be hammered on, then doused in the water tub and shrunk tight. When we quit for dinner, we had fourteen wheels, every one of them as strong and sturdy as stone, leaning against the barn. And by sunset there were fourteen more leaning against them.

Judy and the cultivating crew drove into the yard while Lars was banking his fire for the night, and they'd done fully as well as we had. The corn field was finished, and Judy had found enough fill-in jobs to plug nearly half the soft spots in our hauling schedule.

The whole crew, and even Mrs. Hudson and the children, were as happy as I about the way things were going for us. It was well after dark before we sat down to supper, and when we'd finished eating, no one seemed in any hurry to leave the table. We were all tired enough that it felt good just to sit there, resting our elbows on the table and listening to Jaikus tell stories of the old sod. He was right in the middle of one that had the children laughing when, through the open window,

I noticed the headlights of a car coming along the roadway. A few minutes later there was a knock, and Mrs. Hudson went to answer it. She stepped outside, and for several minutes I could hear the rumble of a man's voice. When she came back, she seemed a bit upset, and told me, "I'm sorry, Bud, after you workin' so hard to get ready and all, but Ted Harmon, he can't commence the thrashing till Wednesday mornin'. The injector on his engine boiler busted, and he had to send off to Denver for a new one."

After pushing so hard to be ready by the first of the week, I was a bit disappointed, and more than a little worried about the note I'd signed. It was due on September 1st, and hauling jobs weren't paid for until they were finished. If the Hudson job took eighteen days, and wasn't started until August 13th, there wouldn't be much leeway for possible breakdowns. Then too, I couldn't be at all sure that Bones wouldn't try to squeeze me if he caught me in a tight corner. Even though I was worried, I didn't want to show it, so as soon as Mrs. Hudson had finished speaking, I said, "Good! That will give us plenty of time to get the teams lined out and put the wagons into tiptop shape."

"You goin' to paint 'em and make 'em look pretty, Bud?" Martha called to me excitedly.

"I hadn't thought much about making them look pretty," I told her, "but maybe we can do something about it now that we'll have some extra time. What color would you like to have them painted?"

Martha looked up the table at me as though she weren't quite sure she'd heard me right. "Color?" she said. "Guess you never seen a brand new wagon. They always have red wheels and green boxes, and bright yella lines on the sides—like little squares with the corner knocked off—and yella stripes on the wheels."

"Well, we'll see what we can do about it," I said. "That is, if you'll go to Oberlin with Judy in the morning, so you can pick us out the right shades of red, and green, and yellow."

The thrashing machine owner's coming sort of broke up

our visit at the table. Within half an hour we'd all turned in for the night, but we were up and on the job by sunrise. And by seven o'clock Judy and Marth were off for Oberlin, to buy paint, brushes, and a few other supplies we needed.

We didn't go back to work on the wheels that morning, but on other parts of the running gears and the bodies, so as to keep plenty of work ahead that Bill, Jaikus, and Paco could do. They bored holes and set bolts and rivets, while Gus made up the metal fittings for them, and Doc sawed stretchers, bolsters, axletrees, brake beams, and whatever new boards were needed for building the sides high enough to carry sixty-bushel loads. I laid flooring, and Lars started forging the coupling rigs and brake assemblies.

By ten o'clock Judy and Martha were back from town, and could hardly take time to change into overalls before they were out to ask where I wanted them to begin painting. Actually, I didn't want them to begin anywhere, because I didn't have much confidence in their artistry, and sticky paint around a job like that is worse than sand in axle grease. But they were so eager that I couldn't refuse them the fun, so opened the can of fire-red enamel, and told them they'd better start in on the wheels we'd finished.

There's an old saying that many hands make light work. I doubt that the number of hands lightened our work that day, but they certainly speeded it. When, at sundown, we knocked off for the day, three completed pairs of fire-red running gears stood in a row, and the finished bodies for them leaned against the side of the barn. The painting wasn't exactly professional looking, but a lot better than I would have expected of two girls, one of them barely an eight-year-old, and Michelangelo couldn't have been more proud of his masterpieces than they were of theirs.

Judy stood back, her head tilted to one side, looking at the gaudy running gears for a few minutes, then called me over to her. "Well, they're pretty all right," she said, "but we might have picked out too bright of a red. It didn't look that light on the sample card, being inside the hardware store and all. I'm sure glad we didn't put none of it on the poles, or doubletrees, or neck yokes. Do you reckon it would look better if we was to put black on the hubs and fellies, and them iron couplers? Just so's to break up the red a little?"

It would have been all right with me if she'd wanted to paint them sky-blue, just so long as it would make her happy, so I told her, "That's exactly what they need, Judy. Then, if you paint the brake pedals and footrests black, our wagons will look as if they'd just rolled out of the factory."

Of course, they wouldn't. No amount of paint could cover up the fact that every one of them was probably older than I, but they'd be solid and strong—and maybe there's no great sin in telling a harmless fib to make somebody you like happy.

When we'd first started rebuilding the wagons I'd planned that, as soon as the cultivating was finished, I'd put Old Bill and Paco to work matching up and training the teams. But with the thrashing put off for a couple of days, there was no rush about the horses, so we worked steadily on the wagons all day Saturday and until noon on Sunday. By that time they were ready for the road, the paint dry, and with enough yellow striping to keep Martha happy.

14

Yimminy! Dat Is Fun!

SUNDAY afternoon was our first playtime, and if a stranger had been watching he'd have thought a wild-west show was going on. Ever since I'd brought home the old saddle and the Manila rope, Paco had been as excited as a little kid waiting for Santa Claus. He'd waxed and polished the old saddle till it shone, picked out the bronc he wanted for his saddle horse, braided hondas into the ends of the Manila, and dragged it until he'd made perfect catch ropes for himself and me. He'd been practicing with a rope every spare minute he could find, but I hadn't dared let him use the saddle for fear it would sour him on helping with the wagons. And for the past week I hadn't had a chance to put a saddle on Kitten.

I didn't say anything about my plans until we'd finished dinner Sunday noon, then looked down the table and said, "Let's get our teams lined up and give them a little workout this afternoon. With that De May job starting in the morning, we'll need three rigs ready to roll, and both we and the horses ought to get in a little practice on cornering and the gulch runs. How about you fellows loading two rigs with about four tons of dirt while Paco and I bring the rest of the horses in from the pasture?"

When Paco heard his name and horses mentioned in the same sentence he jumped out of his chair as though there were a tack in it, and it took only a couple of words of Spanish to send him racing for our ropes and saddles. By the time I reached the corral gate he was there, pulling his rope from the saddle horn and building a loop in it. "Not so fast!" I told him. "Let me catch mine first. I don't want her excited."

I went in quietly, with Kitten's bridle in my hand. As usual she started off for the back corner of the corral, keeping her head turned to watch me, but when I swung a bridle rein above my head she stopped and let me go to her. I slipped the bridle on, stroked her muzzle half a minute, led her out, and told Paco it was his turn.

Paco didn't go at it the way I had, and I think that half his anxiousness for the past few days had been to show me how handy he was with a catch rope. He went in fast, with his loop hanging from his right hand; the coil, bridle, and saddle hanging from his left. His coming into the corral so fast startled the horses and put them into a run, circling, one behind another like the horses on a merry-go-round. At the center of the ring Paco dropped his saddle, swung the loop backhanded, and only once around his head, whirled, and stood it like a rolling hoop in front of the bronc he'd had his eye on from the time he'd first seen it.

Before the mustang could set his feet he'd stepped through the hoop, and Paco had whirled back, closing the loop and hobbling the little bronco at the knees. With one quick jerk, he could have been busted flat on his side, but Paco didn't put him down. Keeping the rope just snug enough to hold the hobble tight, he let the bronc plunge to a stop, went quickly up the line hand-over-hand, flipped a loop around the hobble, and bent it into a half hitch. The whole operation had taken less than a minute, but the horse was as helpless as though he'd been anchored to the ground. In another minute Paco had slapped the saddle and bridle onto him, pulled the half hitch loose, and let the hobble fall to the ground.

I'd been so fascinated by Paco's performance that I hadn't even reached for my saddle, and Kitten had become excited enough by the running of the other horses that she was bobbing her head and dancing. I called to Paco again, telling him to stay where he was until I'd saddled and mounted. Though Kitten was still dancing, she didn't rear when I stepped into the saddle, but sidled around to let me open the gate for Paco. And then the fun began.

Paco had barely hit the saddle before his bronc bogged its head and busted wide open. It was six feet off the ground when it left the corral, and Paco was fanning it with his sombrero as though he were trying to start a fire. He did. Right under me. Old Kitten forgot all about her age, and joined in the fun. She never once reared high with me, or showed any inclination to go over backwards, but she durned near shook every tooth in my head loose. I don't suppose the show lasted more than twenty seconds, but those two little mustangs sure made leather pop for those few seconds, then quit as suddenly as they had begun. I think they'd had as much fun as Paco and I, and once they'd worked off their steam

they handled as if they'd been ridden every day. We let them race the length of the pasture lane, then pulled them to a jog.

Again the horses were in the big gulch, but during harvest they'd lost their fear of the corral, and had learned to expect grain there. The old mares started for the lane at a trot as soon as we'd moved the herd out of the gulch, and the others followed. They gave us no trouble when we held them in the lane to cut back the colts, or when we took them across the yard and turned them into the corral. Then the lid blew off. Putting those two bunches of ornery little mustangs together was like dropping a lighted match into gunpowder. Within less than two seconds heels were flying like corn in a popper, teeth were raking, and chunks of hide and hair sailed through the air like birds.

"All hands bring halters and bridles!" I shouted, at the same time slipping the horn thong, and shaking a loop into my catch rope. "Doc, tend the gate while we snake some of them out of there!"

Paco earned a whole summer's pay in the next few minutes. Without him, I could have had half my horses laid up until the hauling season was all over—and Bones would have had every reason to foreclose on my note. Old Bill earned at least a month's pay, too.

Without missing a single throw, Paco dropped his loop over the neck of one fighting-wild mustang after another, snubbed it tight to his saddle horn, and dragged it, pitching and kicking, to the nearest wagon wheel. There Old Bill would grab an ear, and hold the head down until Gus or Lars could buckle a halter onto it. I snaked out a few myself, but I'll bet Paco got two for every one I did. I've known a lot of men who were good with a catch rope, but never one who could come anywhere close to that Mexican boy. Only Jaikus seemed helpless. He was so afraid of the plunging broncos that he froze in his tracks, and I believe he'd have stood right there if we'd tied one of them to him.

The whole unscrambling couldn't have taken more than eight

or ten minutes, and we got the meanest broncs out first, so no great damage had been done, but when the show was over I could have been wrung out for a dishrag. I hadn't been frightened when the fight was going on, but as soon as it was over my nerves let go, and I sat on old Kitten trembling like a wet dog in January. Even my voice was trembling when I called, "Let's let 'em cool down awhile, and catch ourselves a breather."

That was when Judy proved herself to be a top hand. She hadn't lost her head, as most girls would have, but she must have dumped half a pound of coffee into the pot when she set it over the fire. We'd barely lined up, sitting on the ground with our knees up and our backs against the corral gate, when she came running with the pot and a couple of tin dippers. That coffee was strong enough to have held a spoon straight up, but I never drank any that tasted better.

So much had happened since dinner that it seemed to me it must be nearly time for supper, and as I drank my coffee I was surprised to notice that my shadow was only a foot long. We sat there for maybe fifteen minutes, both to let the horses quiet down, and because I had to make some changes in my plans. Right from the beginning, I'd planned that, with six rigs and six men in the crew, I wouldn't do any driving—not unless someone was laid up for a day, or something of that kind. I'd keep myself loose, so I could watch to see that we ran on schedule, lend a hand where it might be needed, and be free to make arrangements for our moves from one job to another.

Jaikus had knocked that idea into a pile of kindling wood. In that few minutes we'd been in the tangle, he'd proved that he could never handle a four-horse hitch of mustangs. I had to make up my mind whether to pay him off and replace him with a good driver, or to tie myself to a wagon seat. Maybe it was his old-sod stories, or remembering that he'd been just as quick as any one of the others in telling me I could use the money I owed him, but I found myself thinking that I'd as soon give up the whole business as let him go. Even little Billy could have driven the old mares, so I'd take a wagon and let

Jaikus take the mares for his team. He could help us out of the fields with them, and move wagons away from the machine as they were filled.

I was sure the others already knew how useless Jaikus would be to us, and there was no doubt about his knowing it. He didn't take any coffee, and he didn't tell any stories, but sat looking down at the ground between his feet. I waited until the coffee pot was empty, then looked down the line, and said, "Jaikus, will you harness up the bay mares? I'm counting on you to get us out of tight spots with them whenever we get stuck, and I want to find out if they're stout enough to pull one of these double rigs when it's loaded."

Those old mares could have pulled twice as heavy a load there on the rock-hard yard, but I thought it would save Jaikus' pride a bit if he were the first to drive one of the new rigs— and no man can be blamed for being afraid of something he knows nothing about. Jaikus scrambled to his feet before I was through speaking, and hurried away toward the barn, giving the mustangs a wide berth, and calling back, "That I'll do, Bud. It's the both of 'em I'll have harnessed up in a jiffy."

We hadn't taken the old mares out of the corral, or the half dozen other horses that had stayed clear of the battle. Among them was the team Doc had driven the first day of harvest. Next to Jaikus, Doc was the one in whom I had the least confidence as a driver. There were two reasons for it. The first, of course, was that any man who gets into the tanglefoot twice is pretty apt to do it again, no matter how many promises he makes. Secondly, though Doc had been brought up around horses, and though his hands were skillful with tools, they lacked the delicate touch on the reins that was in Old Bill's and Paco's hands.

With high-strung mustangs such as most of mine were, and with the way I planned to run them through gulches, that touch on the reins meant everything. For, in driving a four-horse hitch on the run, the reins are the driver's only means of communicating his will to his horses. The reins, alone, must take the combined place of steering wheel, brakes, and accelerator in a racing car. If the driver's touch is light but postive, a high-strung and intelligent team will respond as accurately as a well-built automobile, but if his hands are heavy, lax, or unsure, his team quickly loses confidence in him, and he's apt to run off the road—always at the most dangerous place. If one of my drivers should have such an accident, with the roads we'd have to travel, he'd probably kill himself and his horses, as well as wrecking the wagons and losing a $250 load of wheat. Then too, a drunk at the end of a pair of reins is fully as dangerous as a drunk behind a steering wheel.

The only reasonably safe thing I could do was to give Doc horses that were steady enough, and level-headed enough, to keep clear of trouble without too much help from him—and the battle in the corral had shown me which ones they were. As soon as Jaikus started off to the barn I got up, called Doc to me, and asked, "Why don't you take that team you drove the first day of harvest for your wheelers? They're heavy enough to hold back a fair sized load on a hill, and it seemed to me they liked the way you handled them. That pair of bays, standing together way over there in the corner, might make you a good snap team. The man I bought them from said he'd used them as leaders on a four-horse hitch, and that they were right good in cornering. I'm going to depend on you for hauling the first load, so I want you to have first choice of teams. Now, if those don't suit you, you pick any teams you'd like."

Doc had always been wary of flying heels, so I knew I was pretty safe in my last offer. He never looked toward the wagons, where the high-strung bunch were tied up, but tried to act as though he were giving each horse in the corral careful study. He walked from one end of the gate to the other a couple of times, turning his head as if he were weighing the good and bad points of each horse, then said, "I reckon those four will do all right, Bud. How about it; you want me to harness 'em now?"

I didn't have too much worry about Gus and Lars. As black-smiths, they must have shod hundreds of horses, and probably some pretty ornery ones. Then too, I'd seen enough in the past month to know they both had the knack of transmitting their own calmness to a horse. Besides, I was sure that, if given their choice, they'd choose the more sensible among the mustangs, that Paco would pick the wildest, and that Old Bill would want those with the most get-up-and-go.

As soon as Doc had gone for his harness, I told the others, "Let's get the rest of these wild cayuses lined up in pairs. Each of you pick the team he wants for his wheelers, and tie them up to the back wheel of a wagon. Then pick your snap team, and tie it to the front wheel. I want you all to have as much choice as I can give you, but I may have to do some switching around to balance the pulling power."

Until I could translate what I'd said for Paco, he looked up at me like the little dog in the advertisements for Victor talking machines, then was off at a run.

Before the men ever started away, I could have come awfully close to telling which teams each one would pick, and for which positions. The only place I'd have missed was on Gus and Lars. They picked the eight I'd been sure they would, but Gus took the steadiest four, and Lars the liveliest. The four left for me were Kitten's four- and five-year-old, and a pair of tough, skittish bays that would weigh about nine hundred pounds apiece.

I'm afraid I acted a bit like Doc. I walked back and forth along the wagons, pretending to size up the pulling power of each team, then told the fellows to go ahead and harness up, that they'd picked the teams better than I could have done it myself. Really, the pulling power didn't make too much difference, since all the horses were fairly evenly matched for size and strength. What counted was that each man believed his team to be the best, for a man can get the best out of horses only if he thinks those horses are the best.

Although Jaikus had only the old mares to harness, and had been the first to start, he was the last to finish. When he led them out of the corral the reins and straps were so mixed up

that they looked like cat's cradles. Paco straightened them out
for him, then we hitched the mares to one of the two loaded rigs.
The traces were barely hooked to the doubletrees before Jaikus
climbed to the high seat, forgetting in his excitement to take
the reins with him. I passed them up, told him to start the
mares slowly, and to try making a full circle of the yard without
stopping. He braced his feet, clutched the reins as though they
were wheelbarrow handles, and began shouting, "Git up! Git
up! Git up!"

The old mares set their feet, leaned against the collars, and
walked away with the heavily loaded wagons as easily as if
they'd been pulling a carriage. To them it was just another job
to be done, but to Jaikus it was a new and thrilling experience.
He sat up as proudly as though he were driving the fire engine
down the main street of Dublin, shouted encouragement to his
steeds, and hauled on one rein, then the other, as if he were
trying to pull a bucket of water out of a well. Almost any other
team would have balked under such handling, but the old mares
were used to Hudson's rough hands, and shuffled around the
yard with their ears flopping.

"That's fine!" I called to Jaikus when he'd completed the
round. "You'll be able to pull us out of many a tight spot before
this hauling season is over. Now suppose you unharness them,
and give them a real good currying and brushing. Horses will
always do best if you keep them well cleaned and brushed."
It was easier for me to tell it to Jaikus than to the rest of
the crew, and I wanted my teams well-groomed while they
were being used on the roads.

I had Gus, Lars, Bill, and Paco hitch their teams to empty
rigs, while Doc and I hitched ours to loaded ones. I knew my
snap team was grass-green, and the most headstrong pair
among the Hudson horses. If hitched to an empty rig, along
with wheelers that were tough and skittish, they might give me
more excitement than I could handle, but they couldn't run
far with a four-ton load—not when I had brakes that were stout
enough to lock the wheels. As for Doc, I didn't want him to

take any gulch at a faster gait than a trot, so had decided to
put him through his practice first, and separate from the other
drivers.

As the men had hitched their rigs up I'd had them form in a
line; Old Bill in the lead, then Paco, Lars, Gus, Doc, and I.
That was the safest method of guarding against any runaways,
and it put Bill in a position to set the pace and patterns. When
we were all ready, I went up and told him, "Take them out in
a stubble field, and give them a good workout on square cornering, figure 8's, and wide circles. You can let them step out a bit
on the figures and circles, so they'll work off a little steam and
ginger before we put them through the roller coasters. While
you're doing it I'll take Doc out to the first gulch we'll have to
cross, and let him and his team try a couple of runs with a
full load. You bring the others out after they've worked up a
good sweat." On the way back to my rig, I stopped just long
enough to tell Doc what he and I were going to do.

When Old Bill led the wagons out of the yard it looked like
a caravan setting out on the Overland Trail. He had his brakes
set tight enough to skid the wheels, but he held the lines lightly,
and kept his fast-stepping broncs to a head-bobbing, prancing
walk. Paco's team, including the bronc he'd ridden to the pasture, tried to buck the harness off, but he kept them tight behind Bill's trailer, and they settled down within a few lengths.
Neither Gus nor Lars had any trouble, and there was none that
Doc, with a heavy load and the steadiest horses in the outfit,
could have.

I was the one who had the trouble. My snap team didn't like
the idea of being out in front, with a pair of strange horses
behind them, and they had no intention of following Doc's
trailer. The moment his rig moved away from in front of their
noses, they tried to make a break toward the corral. Then
when I checked them they tried to turn the other way, and
when I pulled them back they slacked off, letting the singletrees bump them on the heels. That did it! They got the notion
in their heads that the strange team behind them was respon-

sible, and that it was time to defend themselves. I never saw
heels fly so fast and high as those little broncs flung theirs, or
two wheelers that became more panicked. Heels were flying
past their heads like blackbirds leaving a swamp, and they sat
back in the breeching with every ounce of their strength, trying
to escape the barrage. On the hard-packed yard, the wagons
rolled backwards, but not in line. Within less than a minute
the trailer was turned at a right angle, anchoring us solidly.

The only thing that saved me from having a bad accident
and getting some horses' legs broken was Judy's quick thinking.
She and the children had come out to see us off, and when my
snap team went hay-wire she'd run for Hudson's blacksnake.
When I was as tangled up as I could possibly be, she shouted,
"Here, Bud! Here!" and tossed the long whip up to me.

When I'd hung that blacksnake away in the barn, I'd
promised myself that it would never be used on a horse of
mine. It wasn't, but I don't think it missed by more than a
quarter of an inch. I swung it back over my head, and lashed it
out above the snap team's backs, hard enough to make the
cracker thongs pop like pistol shots. There was no need of
biting them with the whip. Hudson had done that so often they
had learned to associate the sound of the cracker with the pain.
Half a dozen good loud cracks were all it took to straighten
them out and throw them into their collars. Once pulling, it
took only an occasional reminder to keep them lined out, but I
was as sparing as possible with the reminders. I was no artist
with a blacksnake, and I didn't want to risk biting one of my
horses with those hide-cutting cracker thongs.

Doc had opened up a good lead, and Bill had turned his little
caravan into the stubble field, before I got out of the yard. Before I caught up I'd worked my team into a good sweat, but
after a week in the pasture that was what the leaders needed,
and with every drop of sweat a bit more of their orneriness
oozed out of them. Doc's hands might not have been the best
in the world on a set of reins, but he wasn't a bad driver. At
the corners he kept his wagons squarely in the roadway. Just

before reaching the sharp rise beyond the Hudson place, he stopped his horses for a breather, then put them into the pull briskly.

I didn't do so well at the corners. At the first one it became evident that my snap team had never been used elsewhere than in the fields, or trained to be driven with reins. It was probable that Hudson had never trained them at all, but used each at the center of a three-horse team, where it could be forced into turning by jockey poles wired to the collar of the horse on either side. Though, in using them on the header, I had replaced the poles with check reins, it hadn't taught the colts anything about reining; they had simply learned to follow along with their teammates at each turn. Worse still, Hudson's rough handling and the rigid jockey poles had toughened their mouths and taught them to move only their heads in answer to any reasonable pull on the bit.

It is natural for any horse to follow a path or roadway, but in turning a corner with a four-horse hitch and a pair of loaded wagons, the lead team can't be allowed to follow the wheel tracks. If they do, the trailer wagon will be turned far too soon, will cut the corner short, and quite probably be overturned in a ditch. If the turn is to the left, the lead team must veer off slightly to the right just as it reaches the corner, pull straight ahead for two lengths, then side-step in a quarter-circle to the left, pulling all the while.

My first turn was to the left, and just as the muzzles of my lead team reached the corner I drew in a little on the right rein, to veer the leaders off and widen the arc for the wagons. I might as well have had my reins fastened to a swivel as snapped to the bit rings of my little lead mustangs. They simply let their heads be turned to the right, while their feet followed the wheel tracks around to the left. I could have yanked them back, as Hudson would have done, but it would only have confused and ruined them. So I drew more firmly on the rein, and the broncs turned their heads until they were nearly touching their shoulders, but kept right on following the wheel tracks.

I could think of only one thing to do—and it worked. I reached for the blacksnake, lashed it out, and made the cracker pop just to the left of the near leader's shoulder. He shied away from the well-known sound, crowding his teammate back to the right, and straining against his collar. From then until the corner was finally turned, I was busier than a cub bear with a hornets' nest. I slung the four reins around my neck, and played them with one hand, as though they were the stops on an organ, while I kept the cracker of the blacksnake popping with the other. I never let the whip come within a foot of either leader, but they would answer a light pull on the rein only if it was accompanied by a pop of the cracker on the opposite side.

It took no more than two or three pops to convince the leaders that I wasn't going to cut them with the whip, so they only veered away from the sound, but the skittish wheelers weren't a bit convinced. Though they answered the reins to either side, they reared and plunged, alternately sitting back in their breeching and lurching into their collars. Actually, they gave me more trouble than the snap team, because I could pretty well fence the leaders in with pops of the whip. It must have taken me ten minutes to turn that one corner, but I kept both wagons on the roadway, although the wheels were almost everywhere but in the tracks. After we were around, I set the brakes and stopped the horses for a five-minute rest, while I stroked their muzzles to quiet them, and to let them know I was well pleased with the job they'd done. And I was pleased. Rough as it had been, it was a good turn for green broncos to make on their first try.

The two other corners I had to turn before reaching the gulch went better, though far from good, and I had to crack the whip only a few times to remind the leaders about obeying a light pull on the reins. Doc was waiting for me, pulled over to the side of the road, a few wagon lengths short of the gulch. I pulled in behind him, set my brakes, hobbled both leaders, and went to climb up on the seat beside Doc.

After explaining that I planned to let the wagons gain a little momentum on the way down, so as to ease the pull up the far side, I said, "Suppose you give it a try, Doc. As you go over the edge, set the brake on your trailer, then hold your lead wagon back just enough to keep it from crowding your horses, but let them pick up a fairly smart trot. Then, near the bottom, turn everything loose, to give your load a good shove as you take it into the uphill pull. If you see that you're going to get stuck before you reach the top, lock down your brakes and hold tight till I've had time to trig the wheels."

Taking a pair of heavily loaded wagons down a hill as steep as that one was, even at a trot, is rather ticklish business the first time a fellow tries it, and Doc was a little over-cautious. He let his wheelers sit back in the breeching, and didn't get his team into a trot until he was halfway down. Then he was late in turning the brakes loose, so he had little momentum when he hit the steep upgrade. His team buckled down and pulled in good shape, but it was a losing battle right from the start. Before we were a third of the way up, the wagons were moving at a crawl, and I had to shout to Doc to set his brakes quick and hard.

If a load starts rolling backward on a steep hill there are only two things for a driver to do; set his brakes, and jump quick. With every foot, the runaway wagons will gain speed, the chances are ten to one that the horses will be dragged off their feet, that the trailer will run off the roadway, and that the whole rig will end up in a tangled heap at the bottom of the gulch.

Doc had no sooner tramped the brakes down, locking them in their lowest notches, than I leaped to the ground, kicked the wires off a fence post, yanked it loose, and jammed it tight behind a wheel. Then I stood there for a minute or two, blowing and telling myself that my high-flown scheme for wheat hauling was nothing but a crazy pipe dream. There was little doubt that the two loads of dirt weighed nearly half a ton more than two loads of wheat would, but Doc's team weighed nearly half a ton more than mine, and at least five hundred pounds more than any other team I had. If they could get only a third of the way up that hill, what chance would a lighter team have? And if I had to cut the load of each wagon down to fifty bushels, or put tote teams in the gulches, there wouldn't be enough profit in the business to pay for wagons and harness, let alone the horses. My success depended entirely on being able to haul an extra twenty bushels on each trip, and in getting over the roads in a hurry.

Of course, I could have unhitched my team, put it in front of Doc's and pulled him to the top of the hill easily enough, but there was no sense in that. What I needed was to find out how much weight my heaviest team could pull up that hill. Fortunately, we'd brought shovels along, so we threw off what we thought to be about half a ton from each wagon. If our guess had been good, that would leave each load at about the same weight as fifty bushels of wheat. When we'd finished, I took the reins myself, set the horses hard into their collars, and released the brakes. With the horses straining every sinew, and with me driving them in a weaving course, they were barely able to pull the lightened loads to the top of the hill.

I let them rest a few minutes, went on a short ways, found a place where I could turn the wagons, and brought them back to the drop-off into the gulch. That time I did the driving, trying to do it just as I told Doc to at the start of our first try. When we reached the spot where we had stalled on the way up, I kicked the brakes loose, crowding the horses into a spanking trot before they reached the bottom of the gulch. The momentum was enough to give us a good start upward, but not enough to do the trick; the horses had to pull with all their strength to haul the loads to the top of the hill.

While we were resting the blowing team, I saw Bill's caravan coming, about half a mile away. I hadn't expected him quite so soon, and wanted Doc to make a run each way by himself, so turned the wagons and passed him the reins. That time, with a little coaching, he made his run just about as I had made mine—as fast as I dared let him learn to make it—and again his team had to strain to reach the top of the hill. He made his run back through the gulch in the same way, but by that time the caravan had arrived, and the drivers stood at the brink of the hilltop, watching the run.

With the afternoon fairly well spent, I wanted to get right on with the practice, but didn't want Doc to see a team put through that gulch at a dead run, so had him unhitch, change wagons with Gus, and go back to the Hudson place. I wasn't too much concerned about Old Bill and Paco, but I was a bit worried about Gus and Lars. They were slow, methodical workmen, and if they tried to put their light teams through that gulch too cautiously, they probably wouldn't do even as well as Doc had done on his first try. Besides, that gulch would probably be an awesome thing to men who were not used to hill or mountain country.

As Gus turned the wagons I climbed to the seat beside him, had him stop at the brink of the hill, and gave him exactly the same instructions I'd given Doc. I might as well have been whistling to the birds. He gathered the four lines between his bananalike fingers, planted a foot solidly on each brake pedal, and shouted, "Hud up!"

His little mustangs hudded. They hit their collars like four battering-rams, and we pitched down the hillside as if we'd been falling into a well. With the broncs almost flying, and with Gus shouting, "Yaa! Yaa! Yaa!" we tore through the bottom of the gulch and rocketed up the far side. The thrust was so great that I doubt the traces were even tightened till we were halfway up, then the teams dug their toes in and snaked us to the top as though the wagons had been practically empty.

I don't often lose my head completely, but I came awfully close to it that time. I hugged Gus around the neck, and told him he was the best driver I'd ever seen in my life.

"Aw, go 'vay," he told me. "I do it yust like you do vit de load from town. Yimminy! Dat is fun!"

It might have been fun for him, but it was certainly a life-

saver for me and my hauling business. When he had made his run back in the same way, I wanted to dance and whoop. There was only one worry left in my mind; the run had been made with Doc's lightened loads. I hurried to my own team, unhobbled the leaders, and climbed to the seat. I knew well enough how risky it was to put my unmatched and untrained broncos down that hill on the fly, but I was so near flying myself that I didn't mind the risk.

If anything, I shouted encouragement louder than Gus, and my little leaders responded with every bit of the fire they'd inherited from old Kitten. They just about had to, or be run over by the wheelers, and by the time we reached the top of the hill every hoof was scrabbling like crazy, but we were still moving faster than a man could walk. When I stopped them for a breather and a pat on the shoulder, I wouldn't have traded any of them for Man o' War. With my lightest team swooping a four-ton load through that gulch as they had, my biggest worries were pretty well behind me.

Lars, Paco and Old Bill used the heavily loaded pair of wagons for their runs, and each of them did fully as well as Gus or I had. Bill made the last run, and when it was finished we shoveled off our loads of dirt, then turned homeward at a brisk trot. Maybe it was the jingling of the harness, or the rhythm of the trotting hoofs, but something made me feel as if I had to sing, even though I can't carry a tune very well, and the songs that came into my head were mostly war songs.

One by one, the others joined in, and it was a good thing that we were far out on the high divide, for Old Bill was the only one of us who could sing both the words and the tunes the way they were supposed to be sung. But we were loud enough to make up for whatever we lacked in pitch or pronunciation. As the wagons rolled briskly down the homestretch and into the yard, we were more shouting than singing, *"We'll KNOCK the heligo, INto heligo, OUT of Heligoland."*

For some reason, that part of that song seemed to fit right in with what we were trying to do in the wheat hauling business and it sort of became our war song.

15

On Our Way to Heligoland

ALTHOUGH we hadn't yet hauled a single bushel of wheat, we had a celebration the evening we first ran the gulch. After supper Judy boiled a big saucepan of taffy, and as soon as it had cooled enough to handle, Mrs. Hudson, the children, and all the rest of us, buttered our hands and took turns pulling it. And as we pulled and snipped it into pieces with a pair of scissors, we sang all the old songs we could think of. Maybe the music wasn't very good, but the fun was.

Before we turned in Doc, Jaikus, and Paco filled feed sacks for the next day, while Gus, Lars, Old Bill, and I talked about the horses, and the runs we were going to make through the gulches. We all knew it would be dangerous business, but we all thought our little mustangs were sure-footed enough to make the risk reasonable. There would always be two big dangers: one that a horse would slip or stumble on the down-hill run; the other that a wagon would stall on a steep uphill pull, that the brakes might not hold, and that it would run backwards, dragging the horses off their feet.

Although horses were seldom shod in that stoneless country, and though there was little possibility that any one of ours had even had its hoofs trimmed, we decided that it would be safest to shoe the whole string. Well-fitted shoes would make them lift their feet higher, cutting down the chance of a stumble. If made with calks, the shoes would eliminate any chance of slipping, and would give a team a much better chance of holding a stalled load until the wheels could be trigged. Then too, we were going to give our horses a tremendous amount of road work, and shoes would be the best insurance against lameness.

Monday morning Judy drove Gus to Oberlin for shoes, nails, and farrier's tools. Lars fired up the forge, and the rest of us harnessed for our first hauling job. It was from the De May place, only five miles from town, and the thrashing rig being used was rated at a thousand bushels a day. With the distance being so short, Bill and Paco could probably have handled the whole job, but I'd promised Doc that he should haul the first load, and I wanted Jaikus to get more experience in driving a team. I had him sweep the dirt out of the rigs we'd used for practicing, disconnect the trailer from one of them, and hitch the old mares to the front wagon. By the time he'd finished, Doc, Bill, and Paco were ready to go, so I saddled Kitten and led my little caravan off to the wars. I don't know how proud Napoleon might have been when he led his army forth to battle, but I'll bet I could have matched him. Old Kitten seemed to catch the spirit of the occasion, she bobbed her head, pranced, and side-stepped as we pulled out of the yard and onto the roadway.

Ever since the Fourth of July we'd been at work by sunup, and I was a little overanxious about getting started that morning. It couldn't have been later than six o'clock when we reached the De May place. The thrashing rig was in place, with the long conveyor wedged between two wheat stacks, and the longer drive belt stretched between the separator and the flywheel of the engine, but the fire under the boiler was still banked, and there was no one in sight. I had Doc set his lead wagon under the grain spout, then took Jaikus on to the long

hill that we'd have to pull three miles before reaching town.
With three rigs on the job, there was no need for the old mares
in helping loaded rigs out of the field; that could be done by
one of the other snap teams.

Even with the old mares and a single empty wagon, Jaikus
nearly panicked when we reached the brink of the big gulch.
He wanted to climb down, lead Kitten, and have me drive the
wagon through. That would have completely ruined him for
any use with horses. What he needed was to gain a little
confidence, and that gulch was the best place for him to gain
it. "No, you're going to do your own driving," I told him. "Put
your foot on the brake, and push it down just enough to keep
the wagon from running down on the mares too hard. They've
probably been through here a hundred times, so you won't
have to worry much about driving them. Just hold them back
enough to keep them out of a trot. I'll ride right beside you,
to give you any help you need."

Without a doubt, it took more courage for Jaikus to make his
drive through the gulch than for any of the rest of us. All the
way to the bottom he had his teeth clamped tighter than a clam-
shell, the reins hauled taut as a fiddle string, and his foot
braced against the brake pedal so hard the team had to keep
the traces tight. He didn't release the brake until they'd started
up the far side, then leaned forward as though he were a jockey
making his bid in the homestretch, fished at the reins as if
he were trying to push with them, and kept shouting, "Git up!
Git up!" at the top of his voice.

The old mares paid no more attention to Jaikus than if he
hadn't been there, and walked through the gulch as if they'd
been on their way to pasture, but Jaikus was elated when he
reached the hilltop. "Fine job!" I told him. "A man that can
drive through that gulch can drive anywhere. Next time, don't
pull on the reins quite so hard. It doesn't help, and would make
your horses' mouths sore."

At the foot of the long grade I had Jaikus unhitch, slip the
bits from the mares' mouths, and empty his sack of feed at

the back of the wagon, so they could munch as they waited for loads to come along. There was no more need of Jaikus being there than there'd have been for a piano player, but he felt that he had a very important job. He assured me that I hadn't a worry in the whole blessed world, that he wouldn't let a single load get stuck on that hill.

By the time I got back to the De May place, the engineer had the fire under the boiler roaring, and was building up a head of steam. Right at seven o'clock the crew drove into the field in a couple of old flivvers. The pitchers shinned to the top of the stacks, and Grampa George Wilson climbed atop the thrashing separator. At a wave of his arm, the engineer opened the throttle, bit by bit, the flywheel began to turn slowly, the wide power belt moved like a long, thin stream of flowing syrup, a dozen or so pulleys, belts, and gears on the separator were set in motion, and the thrashing season had begun.

As the engineer opened the throttle wider, the pulleys, belts, and gears turned faster, the beaters in the maw fed by the conveyor set up a clattering din, the whole machine shimmied and shook—and our little mustangs went crazy. Doc and I were able to hold and quiet his team, but Bill's and Paco's stampeded. With any less skillful men at the reins, they would certainly have run away, but both drivers kept them in a wide circle until they had become used to the uproar and were willing to stand quietly.

When Doc's wagons were loaded, Paco hitched on his snap team to help pull the loads out of the field, and Old Bill drove his lead wagon under the grain spout. I rode beside Doc's wagons all the way to the elevator, not that I was afraid to trust him alone, but to be on hand if he had any trouble. He didn't have a particle, though I doubt that he could have pulled another five bushels out of the deep gulch. At the foot of the long grade, Jaikus hitched his mares on, pushed proudly on the reins as he walked beside them, and made the pull to the hilltop an easy one. At the steep pitch down to the valley, I had Doc set his brakes hard, and keep his horses at a walk. At the elevator they danced a bit when the trap was tilted and the loads dumped, but not enough that he couldn't have handled them alone.

With plenty of wagons, I held the loads down to fifty bushels each, then rode along with Old Bill and Paco on their first trips, but it wasn't necessary. Both went through the big gulch on the fly, took their loads down the pitch to the valley at a slow trot, and had no more trouble than was to be expected when the loads were dumped at the elevator. All there was for me to do was to introduce my men to the scaleman, and show them how to weigh their loads in and their empty wagons out.

As soon as Paco's wagons had been weighed out, I gave Kitten a free rein, and she took me back to the Hudson place at a steady lope. When I got there I found Gus and Lars with both hands full. Our little mustangs weren't in favor of being shod, and they weren't backward about making their feelings known. Lars' wheelers had already been shod when I rode into the yard, but his snap team showed no inclination to suffer any such indignity. Gus was trying to hold one of them by a twitch on its upper lip, while Lars had a hind leg cradled over his thigh, and was trying to trim the hoof. But even the pain of the twitch wasn't enough to keep that little bronc from fighting. Both men weighed well over two hundred pounds apiece, and the mustang no more than seven, but he was more than holding his own.

I'd just unsaddled Kitten and turned her into the corral when I heard a thump, and looked around to see the bronc struggling to get up from the ground. "Sit on his head, so he can't get up!" I called to Gus. "I'll be right there with a soft rope."

When I was a kid on the ranches I'd learned to hog-tie calves for branding, and it seemed to me that might be the best way to shoe our mustangs. When a horse finds that a man has put him into a helpless position, particularly if his head is held down, he has too much intelligence to fight. Then too, if he isn't hurt while he's down, his fear drains away, though he may become panicked with fear while he has his legs under him.

With the bronc already down, it took only a minute to toss a loop around his forelegs, flip the slack around his hind pasterns, pull them together, and lash them tight. From there on the bronc was as easy to shoe as an old plow horse, but Gus and Lars had to hurry right along. It isn't good business to keep any horse, let alone a bronco, tied down too long.

We didn't try to shoe any of the other horses while standing. Either Gus or Lars could make up a set of shoes that would come close to fitting, simply from sizing up a standing horse's hoofs. I'd lead a horse out of the corral, they'd look him over and make up the shoes, then we'd throw and tie him. While I held his head down, they'd trim the hoofs, burn the hot shoes into place, douse them in cold water, and nail them on. Once in a while they had to reshape a shoe, but not very often.

As each horse was let up with his new shoes on, he'd take a few cautious steps, lifting each foot high—like a hen walking in mud. But he'd quickly become used to the added weight, and his gait would be only a little higher than when barefooted. I didn't put them back in the corral after they were shod, but tied each one to a wagon wheel, and brought him a forkful feed. Shoes on a mustang are like brass knuckles on a professional boxer, and if there are calks on the shoes they'll cut like cleavers. Until my broncs had been worked down for a few days, I couldn't risk another battle royal.

By trading horses around, we finished our shoeing at noon on Tuesday, just as Ted Harmon pulled his big thrashing rig onto the Hudson place. Right after dinner I sent Gus and Lars to haul from the De May place, and had Old Bill ride with each of them to be sure they would have no trouble on the steep pitch down to the valley, or in unloading and weighing at the elevator. Then, while Harmon and his crew readied their rig for an early start Wednesday morning, Judy drove me to make my final arrangements for going into full swing at the hauling business.

It was after dark before we sat down to supper that night, but we were as near ready as possible, and I'd hired one more

wagon and driver than we should need, so as to give us a margin
of safety. A load of horse feed had been piled by the roadside
at the foot of both long upgrades, a double load hauled to the
De May place, and Lars had an extra coupler ready for making
a spare tandem rig from two of the hired wagons. I'd hired
five teams of heavy horses, five wagons, and three drivers. One
of the men was to bring his rig directly to the Hudson place at
seven o'clock. The other two would stop to leave a tote team
at the foot of the upgrades, then bring the spare wagons along
to be used as part of a tandem rig.

When we'd finished eating, I said, "Let's go over the whole
setup again, so we won't get crossed up any more than we can
help. Doc, I'm going to put you in charge of the De May job.
Don't try to haul more than fifty bushels to each wagon, and
I don't believe you'll have a bit of trouble in making four trips
a day. The rest of us will haul two double loads a day from
here, and one from the De May place. I'll take one load in for
you at 9:20, Paco will take his at 11:30, and Lars at 1:45. Then
Bill will pick one up at four o'clock, and Gus will be along a
few minutes after five. Tomorrow morning I'll start off with you,
and bring along one of the hired rigs. From then on I'll haul
the last two loads from here each day, letting the last one sit
in the field over night, and hauling it before the thrashers start
next morning. That will give me time in the middle of the day
for whatever running around I have to do.

"We'll let the hired rigs take the first two loads thrashed here
each morning, because they'll be the slowest on the roads. You'll
take the next one, Bill, then Paco, and Gus, and Lars. By that
time the hired teams will be back here to take a load apiece,
and with the thrashing crew taking an hour for dinner, they
won't have another double load ready to go before one-thirty.
That will give Bill plenty of time to get back here, eat his
dinner, and start the second go-round. To save mileage on the
horses, we won't bring any of them to the corral at night, but
feed and groom them at the rigs, haltering them to the front
and back wheels, where they'll be far enough apart that they

can't kick each other. On my last trip, I'll bring in the tote horses, leaving one team at the De May place and bringing the other here. In that way we'll have the hired teams free during the latter part of the afternoons, to take care of any tight spots we may run into.

"Judy, you'll be the busiest one in the crew. With thrashers here you'll have to give your sis a lot of help with the cooking, and you'll have to drive the wheels off the old Maxwell. No two of us will go to work, get done, or eat our dinners at the same time. You'll have to take us out to the rigs every morning, fetch each one his grub whenever he has time to eat in the middle of the day, and bring each one back here when he's finished with his last load. Besides that, it will be your job to keep us in fresh meat and groceries, and to be trouble shooter on the roads, so as to watch that we all stay on schedule. If this thing works, as tight as I've got it set up, we'll just about have to run on a timetable to keep pace with the two thrashing rigs. Let's turn in early, and be ready to knock the heligo out of the hauling business when morning comes."

Although neither rig would begin thrashing before seven o'clock we were all harnessed and ready to go by six, but Lars wouldn't take his first load until eleven, so I told him to couple the two wagons from the tote teams together, and take them to the De May place as soon as they were ready. Then I left Bill in charge at the Hudson place, and went with Doc to the De May job, where one of the hired haulers was to meet us at seven. He was there a little before time, and so were Grampa George and his crew. Right at seven o'clock, a golden stream of wheat began pouring into Doc's lead wagon, and by eight he had started away for the elevator. I pulled my wagons under the grain spout as he pulled his out, and when Lars brought the extra rig, Grampa George had him set it on the opposite side of the machine, ready to catch grain when my rig was loaded.

As soon as Judy had come to take Lars back I climbed onto the separator and shouted to Grampa George above the clatter,

telling him to load Doc's wagons with only fifty bushels apiece, but to give the rest of us sixty bushel loads. He looked at me as though he thought I'd lost my senses, and shouted back, "Ain't you been over the roads yet, boy? I doubt me you can make it with a hundred to a double load—not with them little ponies. It would take six stout horses to pull a hundred and twenty bushels out of them gulches."

"I'm going to risk it," I shouted. "I've got two heavy tote teams along the road to pull us out if we get stuck."

Grampa George reached down and reset the gong on the tally register to strike at sixty instead of fifty, but he was still shaking his head when I climbed down.

The golden stream of grain poured from the spout without a moment's letup, and kept me busy spreading the load evenly in the wagon. When I heard the gong strike I held my shovel tight against the end of the spout, and swung it back to the trailer. It was just 9:20 by Grampa George's watch when the gong struck again, and he switched the stream to the empty wagons.

I'd run the big gulch, hooked on the tote team, and was half-way up the long hill when I met Doc coming back with his empty rig. As we passed we both bawled, "Yip, we're on our way to Heligoland," but neither of us stopped.

In every spare minute I'd been able to find during the past couple of days, I'd been harnessing my teams, driving them out to the first corner, and giving them a little more practice in making the turns. They'd improved considerably, but still weren't very handy at it, and I had five corners to turn as I came down from the divide, through the village, and pulled in at the elevator. I expected a little trouble on those corners, and had it, but it was nothing to the excitement I had in going down the main street of the town.

My little leaders seemed to have a deep-seated distrust of urban environment, and were violent in their protests against my efforts to force them into it. Several times, in trying to turn back, they doubled around so far I could look them in the faces. Only their fear of the blacksnake kept them straightened around where they belonged, and I often had to pop the cracker within an inch or two of their heads. It must have taken me a full fifteen minutes to run that one-block gauntlet, and the tracks of my wagon wheels looked as if they'd been left by squirming angleworms. To help things along, Bones came out of the bank when I was in the thickest of the battle, and shouted, "How you getting along, Son?" I couldn't trust myself to answer him.

I had a little more trouble in convincing my snap team that the driveway through the elevator wasn't the road to perdition, but once they'd passed over it they seemed to accept their fate.

Though they kept turning their heads from side to side, looking for something to spook at, they trotted right along as I drove them back through town. We'd just passed the church and started up the steep climb from the valley when we met Paco coming down. Gus was hitching on his second tote team, three and a half miles from town, when I passed him, and when I came to the sharp rise just before reaching the Hudson place, Jaikus was unhitching the old mares after giving Lars a pull out of the field. At each passing, we shouted that we were going to knock the heligo out of Heligoland, but I didn't stop. There was no room in our schedule for visiting.

It was eleven-thirty when I pulled up at the thrashing rig. With my next load not due out until five o'clock, I unharnessed my horses, fed them, and had the engineer give three toots on his whistle—the call for Judy to come with the Maxwell. She must have driven me at least a hundred miles between then and five o'clock—carrying dinner buckets, checking loads on the road, and going to Oberlin for six two-dollar watches.

Gus and Lars had gold watches, so I didn't buy any for them. Of course, Jaikus didn't need one, but I didn't want him to feel left out, and the rest of us just about had to have them. My schedule was so tight that the thrashers would have had to stop their machines if we'd fallen as much as fifteen minutes behind time, but that wasn't the main reason for my buying the watches. It was just the opposite. Everyone was so over-anxious that he was hurrying his horses too much, and not giving them enough time to rest after hard pulls. That kind of driving will break horses down much quicker than overloading or ex-cessive mileage, and I had to guard against it. To spare our horses as much as possible, each run had to be so accurately timed that a round trip wouldn't vary by more than five minutes. If a man lost time on the way to town, or if he had to wait at the elevator, he could make up for it on his way back with empty wagons. But there was no sense in wearing the teams down by getting back fifteen or twenty minutes too early, and the men needed watches for timing themselves. Judy needed one as badly as the rest of us, for part of her job was to keep a check on all hands, and to bring me word of any trouble or falling behind schedule.

It is seldom that a new and closely scheduled job runs smoothly on its first day, and it is almost never that two such jobs can be dovetailed together and still run smoothly, but ours did. Neither thrashing rig had a minute's breakdown all day, both turned out their full capacity of grain, and there was never a time when we didn't have wagons waiting to catch it. My greatest trouble was to keep the crew from rush-ing too much, or from failing to give their horses long enough rests after hard pulls.

At five minutes after five I pulled away from the rig on the Hudson place with the last load to be hauled for the day. Though there would be another one thrashed, it would sit in the field until I hauled it away at seven o'clock the next morn-ing. With mine being the last load, there was no need for me to hurry. I ran the gulches fast, but gave my horses long rests on the far side, and others after pulling each of the long up-grades.

It was quarter of seven before I reached Cedar Bluffs, the stores were all closed, there was no one on the street, and my little leaders went down it without the slightest bobble. After my loads had been dumped and my empty wagons weighed out, I waited for Doc to bring in the last load from the De May place. He came in right at seven o'clock, and was weighed out by seven-ten, but the scaleman was a little annoyed. Seven was closing time for the elevator, and he was a bit grumpy about being kept overtime. All it took to keep him happy was to tell him we'd let the last load from the De May place sit in the field over night, and Doc would bring it at seven in the morning instead of seven at night. It really made an easier day for Doc. On the new schedule, he'd pull his first load out at six in the morning, and be all finished for the day by half-past-three.

Although the tally registers on the thrashing machines were fairly accurate, they measured by volume, and were only a guide to go by in loading. At the elevator the measure was entirely by weight, and I would be paid in accordance with the elevator tally. Before the wheat was dumped into the pit, an exactly measured sample was taken from each wagon, weighed in a tester, and examined for grade. If the kernels were small and shriveled, the tester might show that it ran no more than fifty-four or -five pounds to the volume bushel, while exceptionally good grain might run as high as sixty-four or -five, and regardless of bulk, sixty pounds was counted as a bushel.

After Doc's wagons had been weighed out, the scaleman gave me our tally for the day, and it totaled 2,305 bushels— 1,270 from the Hudson place, and 1,010 from Grampa George's rig. On the way back, Doc led the first tote team on to the De May place for the night, and I led the second one on to the Hudson place. I barely had the horses unharnessed, tied to the wagon wheels, and fed, before Judy stopped to pick me up on her way home with Doc.

Though the thrashing crew had long since eaten supper and gone home, my whole crew had waited so we could eat together. It was one of the best evenings we'd ever had, more like a celebration than supper, and when we sang, *"We're on our way to Heligoland,"* we could have been heard from a mile away.

16

Home on the Dry Divide

AFTER our first big day of hauling, Judy and I sat up late, figuring out the exact schedules, writing a copy for each driver, and making entries of the day's business in our books. With our hauls being eight miles from the Hudson place, and five from De May's, our day's hauling figured out—at one and a half cents a bushel per mile—to $228.15. That seemed a lot of money to earn in a single day, but we couldn't be sure there was any profit in it. My cost for wages for my own crew that day had been $70, there had been another $43 for hired drivers and teams, and the grub and horse feed would amount to another $25, leaving a balance of only $90.15. Then too, I was already in debt $2,606 for horses, harness, wagons, repair materials, supplies, and groceries, as well as $840 that had piled up for wages since the last day of harvest. It didn't take much figuring to show that we'd have to get in a bit over thirty-eight days of hauling at that rate for me to get myself out of debt.

I could see only two bright spots—and one that wasn't so bright. The bright ones were that there was still one load in the field that would have been hauled on any but our first day, and that we'd had no use for one of the rigs I'd hired. The rig and driver had cost me $11, with another $1.50 for grub and horse feed, and the load in the field would bring $14.40 for hauling. The dark spot was that I lost money on hired rigs. With big, slow horses, the best a driver could do was to haul two fifty-bushel loads eight miles in a day. The hauling brought in $12, and my cost was $12.50.

Our second day went fully as well as our first one. I was away with my first load by quarter of seven, took my second from Grampa George's rig at 9:20, and was back at the Hudson place by eleven o'clock. Somewhere along the way I had passed every one of my drivers, and each one was exactly on schedule. With things going that smoothly, there was no need for running the wheels off the old Maxwell, and with me free for six hours in the middle of the day, there was no need of keeping Judy on the run. Except for taking us to the rigs in the morning, and bringing us in at night, it was better for her to stay at the house and help her sister, particularly with a thrashing crew to feed as well as the rest of us. When we'd first come to the place, Doc had thought there would be another Hudson before harvest was over, but Judy had told me the baby wasn't due for another month at the earliest. Still, Mrs. Hudson was in no condition to be doing the cooking for sixteen men, while trying to take care of five small children.

Until it was time to harness for my five-o'clock trip, I carried out the dinner buckets, visited a few minutes with each driver as he ate, drove to The Bluffs for a little visit with Bones—and to be sure all the wagons were rolling on schedule—then got better acquainted with Ted Harmon and Grampa George. The old man still couldn't figure how we were getting 120-bushel loads through the gulches with our little mustangs, but I didn't tell him. If I had, he'd have been positive that I'd lost my senses. On my trip to town I'd stopped at each gulch to watch one of my drivers go through, and each one had done the trick as handily as if he'd done it all his life.

My own horses pricked up their ears as we approached the brink of each gulch, then laid them back flat to their necks, and raced through as though they found as much thrill in it as I did.

That second evening I never had to lay a hand on the black-snake. By that time my leaders were cornering nearly as well as any of the others, and neither shied nor danced when going through the town and into the elevator. It was just after 6:30 when I weighed my empty wagon out, and when the scaleman gave me my tally for the day, it totaled 2417 bushels. I picked up both tote teams on my way home, leaving one at the De May place, and taking the other on to the wagon circle on the Hudson place. When Judy picked me up, I took the blacksnake along, and hung it back in the barn.

That evening when Judy and I figured up and entered the books things looked a little better. We'd hauled 1425 bushels from the Hudson place, and 992 for Dr. De May, for a total earning of $245.40, so we had nearly $120 to help pay off the debts.

By the third day our hauling had settled so well into a pattern that there was no longer any need for my running back and forth to see that we kept on schedule. Each man knew the exact minute he was due to pull away from a thrashing rig, when he should reach the elevator, and when he should be back. Of course, the machines didn't turn out exactly the same number of bushels every hour, so some of our loads were a few bushels short, and others a few over. About all there was for me to do, beside delivering my three loads a day, was to lug out dinner buckets, and bawl, *"We're on our way to Heligo-land,"* when I passed one of my rigs on the road.

By our fourth day I felt sure enough that the business was going to be successful that I dared go still further in debt, and Bones agreed with me enough to lend me another thousand dollars. That time I didn't have to tell him what kind of a note to make out, and he didn't object to making it for sixty days— so long as the interest was 8%.

Maybe it's the Scotch blood in me, or maybe it's because I was born in New England, but it always hurts my feelings to see profits getting away. And profits were getting away in my hired teams. Besides, I knew from my first buying trips right where I could get more mustangs just about as good as the ones I already had. I didn't need anything very good for tote horses, since we didn't require a lot of extra pulling power for getting up the long grades, so fairly cheap horses would do as well as any others, just so they were willing pullers. At Oberlin I could find almost any kind and condition of wagons and harnesses I wanted. By the end of the week I'd invested the whole thousand: $400 for four good mustangs, $200 for four good-enough tote horses, $200 more for four wagons that didn't need any rebuilding, $20 for coupler steel, and $180 for four sets of stout harness.

A boy who had been driving one of the hired rigs was real handy with a four-horse hitch, and had nerve enough for running the gulches. I didn't think he should have as much as the men who had stuck by me all through harvest, who had never drawn but a few dollars of their pay, and who had offered to let me use the rest of it. But when I told the boy I'd pay him $6 a day, right through to the end of the hauling season, and whether or not we worked every day, he was glad to take the job. With forty-three or -four more days of hauling contracted ahead, I could save enough in team hire to pay for the new horses and wagons. And if I could keep the rig busy every day, hauling 120-bushel loads, it would make me nearly $600 in cash profits besides.

Each noon when I took a driver his dinner bucket, I looked over his horses from hoofs to muzzles, watching for any sign of breaking down—any swelling of a leg that might indicate a strained tendon, any lump on a hock that might develop into a spavin or thoroughpin, or any excessive loss of weight. During harvest we'd worked the Hudson horses into the lean, hard, toughness of well-trained racing Thoroughbreds, and the week at pasture had put them into prime condition. But some of the new mustangs had been carrying a few pounds of soft flesh when I'd bought them, and with forty-two fast miles on the road every day, half of it under heavy load, they were losing weight faster than I liked.

I couldn't be positive that part of the loss wasn't due to my feeding them the weedy wheat hay we'd cut from the borders of the fields, and I couldn't risk taking any unnecessary chances. Unless those horses were kept in tiptop condition, I'd be broke and out of business. Wheat, together with straw that has some sap left in it, isn't bad feed for horses doing ordinary work. But when they are being overworked they should have feed strong enough to fully balance the energy they're spending—and in that country nothing better than oats and third-cutting alfalfa hay could be found. At the beginning of my second week I bought fifty bushels of oats, and had a farmer from the valley bring us two loads of freshly cut alfalfa hay. From then on, each horse was fed ten quarts of oats a day, together with as much hay as he would clean up, and was watered at least three times.

Although we had lots of days when we ran full tilt, we had others when we were a few loads short; because a thrashing rig broke down for an hour or two, had to move from one field to another, or when we were finishing with one of the smaller jobs and starting another. Then we lost a couple of days because of rain, but most of the time we had all the business we could handle. Within a week after we'd started hauling, our rigs— and our battle hymn—were known throughout the whole surrounding country, and a day seldom passed without some farmer stopping me on the road, or coming to see me, about hauling for him when he started his thrashing. Of course, I couldn't take any more big jobs, but I picked up enough fill-in hauling to give my horses all the work I dared put them to. Originally I'd thought that forty to forty-two miles a day would be as much as they could stand, but as they toughened and hardened I raised the limit to forty-five, and they throve on it. Sometimes our jobs overlapped a bit, so I had to hire a few extra teams and drivers, but there was no profit in it, so I kept it down as much as I could.

There is little doubt that the last week in August was the happiest Mrs. Hudson had ever had. By that time we knew that her wheat was going to yield a good full twenty-two bushels to the acre, and the rain we'd had at the first of the month would assure her a corn crop. After we'd had a talk with Bones, and I'd shown him the tally slips, she bought a nice little house in town and a new Maxwell. Then she left the children with her folks, and spent the whole week shopping for furniture and all the things she'd need for her new home, but she wouldn't leave the ranch until the thrashing had been finished.

The day we'd talked with Bones, the landlord had called on Mrs. Hudson in the evening, and offered to lease me the whole place for the next year. I didn't want the wheat land, but made a deal with him to lease the pasture and buildings. Then I made a deal with Mrs. Hudson to harvest her corn crop in exchange for her cows and the old Maxwell.

Mrs. Hudson wasn't going to move any of the junk furniture from the house, and I didn't want it either. But with fall coming on, I did want to move my crew inside, so the next morning I gave Judy a check for $200, and told her, "I can't afford to spend a lot of money for furniture, but I'd like to fix the house up enough that we can be comfortable in it till the hauling season is over. Suppose you take a ride over to Oberlin and see what this will buy us in surplus Army cots, and a little decent secondhand furniture: chairs, a table, and a couple of dressers with drawers enough to hold our clothes."

"Well," she said, "this will be enough to get the stuff we'll need, but I don't know if I can find it all in one day."

"That's all right," I told her. "Take as many days as you want. You won't have much time anyway, not with your sis away most of the time and thrashers to cook for."

Judy took me at my word. As soon as she'd taken us to work each morning, she'd drive away, come back at noon to feed the thrashers and bring us our dinner buckets, then drive away for a couple of more hours. In the middle of the week I asked her how she was getting along, but she didn't seem to want to talk about it, and just said she hadn't had time to find the best bargains yet.

There had been several times when I'd needed the old Maxwell, so I told her, "Don't worry too much about getting the best bargains. I have an idea you can buy everything we need at the Army and Navy Surplus store. They have folding chairs, and tables, and cots. Foot lockers would do as well as dressers, just so each one of us has some place to keep his clothes. You pick out the stuff, and I'll send a wagon over to haul it for you."

"Hmmmf!" she sniffed. "They're robbers over to the Army-Navy store. Two hundred dollars wouldn't go no place there. And besides, there's no sense getting the stuff out here till sis moves into her new house. When do you reckon the thrashing will be finished?"

"Saturday," I told her, "unless there's a breakdown."

"You hauling Sunday?" she asked.

"Not from Harmon's rig," I told her. "It will take him all day Sunday to move to the north divide, but Grampa George will be thrashing, so Doc and I will haul from his rig."

Judy looked a bit bewildered for a few seconds, then asked, "Couldn't somebody else work in Doc's place? I was counting on him to help me Sunday."

I didn't exactly like to have Judy pick Doc instead of me for helping her buy furniture. It wasn't that I was jealous; it just hurt my feelings a little bit, so I said, "Okay, if you want Doc you can have him. Paco and I can take care of the hauling." After that evening I didn't mention furniture to her, and she didn't mention it to me, either.

It was after four o'clock on Saturday before Ted Harmon finished the thrashing on the Hudson place. I took the last load to the elevator, waited for the operator to make up the final settlement statement, and went to meet Mrs. Hudson at the bank. She had been with Bones and her attorney all afternoon, examining the claims outstanding against her, figuring the accumulated interest, and writing the checks with which to pay them. After I checked the final elevator statement with my delivery slips, we figured up the thrashing and hauling, and found that Mrs. Hudson's share of the wheat crop, after paying every penny she owed, would leave her nearly $14,000. My check for the hauling was $3,379, but after paying off my $2,000 note, it left me only $36.59 in my bank account that I didn't owe to my crew—and I still owed a $1,000 note for the last horses and wagons I'd bought.

It was well after dark before we finished at the bank, and Mrs. Hudson went to her new home. I drove to Grampa George's thrashing rig, and Judy came to pick me up by the time I'd unharnessed and fed my horses. Neither of us mentioned furniture on the way back to the house, and maybe I was a little bit stuffy. For the past three days she'd been away somewhere with the Maxwell when I needed it badly, and three or four times I'd found her and Doc with their heads together.

Of course, with Mrs. Hudson no longer on the ranch, Judy had to move back to her folks' house. After we'd finished entering the books that evening, I told her there was no need of her coming out before eight o'clock the next morning; that I'd cook breakfast for Paco and myself, and that we'd ride saddle horses to the rig. With a day off, the rest of the crew would probably sleep late. She'd always put the books away and filed the tally slips when we finished, but that night she left it for me to do, and hurried away to the Maxwell. I heard the motor backfire and start within two minutes, but Judy didn't drive away until I'd finished the filing and blown out the lamp in the kitchen.

She was just leaving the yard when I started for our camp, and in the starlight I saw the dark outline of a man going around the corner of the barn. I knew from the size and shape that it was Doc. There was no reason he couldn't talk to Judy if he wanted to, or she to him, but for some reason it made me a bit edgy. I killed a few minutes by going to the corral, more to cool down than to see if the men had fed the horses that wouldn't be working next day. By the time I reached the camp Doc was rolled in his blanket, and lying as still as if he'd been asleep for hours.

I was a little slow about going to sleep that night, but not about waking up the next morning. The stars were just turning pale with the coming of dawn when the clattering of the old Maxwell wakened me. There was no sense in getting up that early, when we didn't need to be on the job till six-thirty, but I shook Paco, and we dressed. When we came around to the yard, an oblong of yellow light was streaming from the kitchen window, and for the first time I ever heard her, Judy was singing as she cooked breakfast. From what I'd seen the night before, I had a pretty good idea why she was singing, and it didn't make me very happy. I don't think I said a word to Paco as we fed and watered the horses, then washed up for breakfast.

I was even less happy when we went in to eat. Judy had breakfast on the table, and was humming as she stowed grub into a paper sack. "You'll have to make out with a cold lunch this noontime," she told me. "I've got a lot of things to do today, and won't have time to cook a hot dinner and fetch it to you."

I didn't mind eating a cold lunch, and at any other time it wouldn't have bothered me a particle, but that morning it did. I felt as though I were being treated like a step-child in my own house. I tried not to show that I felt a bit grumpy, but I couldn't think of much to say during breakfast, and I don't think we were at the table more than ten minutes. Then, when I saddled Kitten, she acted as ornery as I felt. I thought I'd handled her as carefully as always, but when I stepped into the saddle she buck jumped for a quarter mile before she'd quiet down.

The whole day was one of those sour ones. Grampa George was grouchy because his men had been to town Saturday night, got into the tanglefoot, and were doing a poor job of pitching. The scaleman at the elevator was peevish because he'd planned on having that Sunday off. And I must have let some of my own peevishness get through the reins to my horses; they snapped at each other all day, cornered like a bunch of half-broken colts, and spooked when there was no reason for it.

It was six-thirty, and sunset, when I delivered my last load at the elevator, and seven-thirty by the time Paco and I had driven our rigs home. When we drove into the yard, the place seemed deserted. There was no light in the house, and no one came to help us unharness. The only way I could account for it was that the whole crew had gone to town for the day, and that Judy hadn't even bothered to come back and cook supper for us. We unharnessed, put the horses into the corral, washed at the windmill, and went to the house to get ourselves something to eat. The kitchen door was closed, there was a peculiar smell about it, and when I pushed it open Judy sang out, "Surprise! Surprise!"

If ever a man was surprised, I was the one. And if ever a man was ashamed of himself for being a jealous, sulky fool, I was that one, too. Just as Judy sang out, Doc lighted a lamp, and I could hardly believe I was looking into the same kitchen I had left so grumpily that morning. The whole crew was standing there, spattered with paint and laughing at my bewilderment, and the only thing I could recognize was the old cook stove. Even that had been blackened and polished till it sparkled. The walls, woodwork, and ceiling had been painted, the floor scrubbed with lye until it was bleached almost white, and there were checkered curtains hung at the windows. Eight solid oak chairs sat around a big table that was covered with a tablecloth to match the curtains, and set with brightly patterned dishes and sparkling silverware. At the far end of the kitchen there was an old-fashioned, ornate sideboard, with more dishes showing through the glass-paned doors. Beside it there was a work table, with four new pine shelves bracketed to the wall above, each loaded with groceries, pots, and pans.

Judy was fairly jumping with excitement, and the rest of the crew wasn't far from it. I'd barely had time to look around before she took my arm with one hand, the lamp with the other, and told me, "Come see the rest of it, Bud, but don't get against the paint; it's still kind of wet."

When she led me through the doorway to the next room, I might have thought I was stepping into my grandmother's parlor. The walls and ceiling had been freshly papered, the woodwork painted, three braided rugs lay on the well-scrubbed floor, and the furniture was of about the same vintage as the sideboard in the kitchen. There was a horsehair sofa, a Morris chair, two rockers, and a six-sided center table, with a fringe-shaded, round-wick lamp hanging from the ceiling above it.

"There wasn't no sense in having two bedrooms for only men," Judy told me, "so we fixed this one up for a place to sit down after supper—it getting dark so early now, and all. Then this other one's the bunkhouse."

As she spoke, she opened the door to the third room, and led me in. It, too, had been freshly papered and painted. Two double bunks had been built against each side wall, and there was an old-fashioned dresser at each end of the room—one of them with a mirror, washbowl, and white pitcher. And at the center there was a narrow table, with another round-wick lamp hanging above it, and a chair at each end. "Without we'd used both rooms for sleeping, there wouldn't have been no place for seven cots, like you said I should get," Judy told me, as she led me to one of the bunks, "but these will sleep real good, 'cause I got springs for 'em, and thick pads." She turned the blanket back to show me the bed, made up with sheets, a pillow, and pillowcase.

"For heaven's sake," I asked, "how did you folks get all this done in a single day, and where did you get the money to do it with?"

"Stuff like this old furniture don't cost next to nothing if you look in the right places for it," Judy told me. "Old folks put it in their attics when their kids grow up and they move into smaller houses, and they're glad to get a couple of dollars out of it. That's how we had money enough for the springs and pads and lumber and stuff."

"Even at that, I can't see how you did it all in a single day," I said.

Judy grinned and told me, "We didn't. We been working on it ever since Sis took the children down home, so they wouldn't

blab and spoil the surprise. I've been having the big stuff fetched
to our place down home when I bought it, and Bill and Jaikus
hauled it out last night when you was settling up with Sis and
Bones at the bank. Then with Gus and Lars not going to work
till nearly noon, and Doc home by four, we've had plenty of
time for carpentering and paper hanging. Of course, we couldn't
do no painting till you left this morning, and I was scairt we
wouldn't get it all done 'fore you come home tonight. How
do you like it, Bud?"

For some reason my throat had swollen enough that I couldn't
talk very well, but they all knew how happy I was, though only
I knew how ashamed.

17

Ragtag No More

From the time Judy fixed up the house until the end of the hauling season, she worked far longer days than any of the rest of us, but she wouldn't have it any other way. Every morning she'd drive out from town in time to have our breakfast on the table by 5:30, she was never late with a dinner bucket at noon, and it was often 8:30 before we'd finished our bookkeeping in the evenings. We could have cooked our own breakfasts without any trouble, and I really didn't need her for the bookkeeping, but she'd never leave for home until the last entry had been made, and as the figures piled up her excitement grew right along with them. Just as a youngster will count off the days remaining until Christmas, she counted off the days till our profits would be enough to pay off my second note, the grocery and feed bill, the hire of extra teams, and all the wages earned by the crew. Whenever we struck a day without enough work to keep every rig going full time, she grieved about it, and blamed herself for not having found some fill-in job to keep the rig busy.

It was the third Friday evening in September when we went over the top. As near as Judy and I could figure—counting the bank balance and amounts due for hauling that was already completed—every penny I owed could be paid, and there'd be a balance of $34.27 left over. She jumped up from the table, dancing and calling to the crew that we'd already knocked the heligo out of Heligoland. I wanted to shout right along with her, but I didn't let myself do it. It wouldn't have been the right thing for a businessman to do. But I did tell the crew that we'd go to Oberlin on Saturday night and celebrate.

All day Saturday I worried about our celebration. Ever since the time I'd had Doc dunked in the watering trough, I'd kept the whole crew away from Oberlin, just to keep him from going on another binge, and I hated to run the risk now that we were heading into the homestretch. A dozen times during the day I thought about having a talk with Doc, but I didn't do it. For a kid like me to go preaching to a man of his age would have been foolishness, and I couldn't tell him I'd fire him if he got into the tanglefoot, because it would have been a straight-out lie. Of course, I couldn't let him touch a pair of reins again until I was positive he was cold sober, with all the shakes gone out of his hands, and until I knew that he didn't have a bottle stashed away somewhere, but I couldn't fire him—not with me making big profits and his having stuck by me the way he had.

I told Judy not to bother about cooking any supper that night, so when I took my first load to the elevator I phoned the restaurant in Oberlin, telling them to have nine of the best steaks in town ready for us at seven o'clock. Then I rented a flivver from one of the pitchers on the thrashing crew, so we wouldn't overload the old Maxwell. By leaving three loads in the fields, we had plenty of time to wash up, shave, and be at the restaurant on time. When we went in we must have looked like a gang of hoodlums who had abducted the banker's daughter. Judy had gone home late in the afternoon to dress up in her prettiest clothes, while the rest of us were in blue shirts and overalls.

The supper was a good one, and since it was a celebration, I ate steak right along with everyone else. As soon as we'd fin-

ished, I fished out my checkbook, and said, "I'm taking Judy
to the movies if she'll let me. We'd sure like to have you fellows
come along if you'd like to, or do anything else you'd rather,
just so long as we're all back at the cars by midnight. How
much money would you like to draw?—all or any part."

I'd always paid our new man every Saturday, and had already given him his check. Gus and Lars shook their heads,
Jaikus and Bill took ten apiece, and Doc took twenty. Paco had
never had a check or drawn a dime, but I gave him a ten-
dollar bill from my pocket. Then everyone just sat, saying
nothing and looking uncomfortable, so I was pretty sure they
didn't want to spend the evening in a movie, but to break it
up, I asked, "How about it, Judy? Would you go to the movies
with a bum in overalls, or is there something else you'd rather
do?"

I must have put a little emphasis on the *you'd*, because Judy
had barely said she'd like to go before Old Bill told me, "I'd
sure like to go along if you hadn't rather to take her alone,
Bud, but I got an errand I'd kind of like to run first . . . it
being the only time we've been to the big town, and all."

All the others—except Doc and Paco—said the same thing,
then they all left the table and went out while I was paying the
waiter. At the door, Old Bill called back, "See you in front of
the theater in about fifteen minutes."

I tried to make some pleasant chatter as I hooked Judy's arm
under mine and walked her up the main street toward the
theater, but I wasn't a bit happy. I didn't have to be very smart
to know that my crew had been doing a little conniving behind
my back, and that Paco was in on it, right up to the knees. What
was more, I had a durned good idea as to what the conniving
had been about, and that it could easily blow my hauling business to smithereens. It would be bad enough to have Doc get
into the tanglefoot, and with his having drawn twenty dollars
there wasn't much doubt of his doing it, but if he got the rest of
the crew pickled I could be out of business.

Until that night in front of the theater, Judy and I could

usually find plenty to talk about, but that night we both acted as if we were tongue-tied, and for the same reason. Fifteen minutes passed, and five more, and another five was nearly up when I saw our whole crew come out of the department store across the street, looking as if they were Santa Claus' little helpers. Everyone of them was lugging packages, and Doc had what looked to be a megaphone in one hand. They trooped across the street like a bunch of kids just out of school, Paco in the lead, with his teeth gleaming and his eyes sparkling. He crossed the sidewalk in a single bound, swept off his sombrero, bowed low to Judy, held out his package, and said haltingly, "Forrr . . . ourrr . . . ," then ran out of English words and finished joyfully, "amada señorita."

The others left no doubt that Judy was, "our beloved girl."

Every one of them had brought her a box of candy, along with a bottle of perfume, a blouse, a half dozen handkerchiefs, or some other pretty trinket—and Doc's megaphone turned out to be a dozen hothouse roses.

I don't even remember what the movie was about, but we had ice-cream sodas before we left town, and we sang all the way home—I loudest of all.

At noon on the Monday after our celebration, Bones sent word that he wanted to see me right away. I couldn't imagine what he wanted to see me about in such a hurry, since my note wasn't due for another twenty days, and he could see from looking at my account that I had plenty of money to pay it, but I cranked up the old Maxwell and drove to The Bluffs.

When I went into the bank Bones came hurrying to the little gate in the railing, swung it open, and said, "Come in, Son! Come right in! I've got some mighty good news for you." He led the way to his desk, waved his hand toward the chair beside it, sat down, and pulled a roll of papers from a pigeonhole.

I'd have had to be awfully stupid not to smell a mouse, but I sat down, grinned, and said, "Let's have it. If there's anything I like to hear, it's good news."

Bones leaned toward me confidentially, and said, "Son, I've been doing a lot of worrying about you in the last three or four weeks. Sure, you've done fine with your hauling business, better'n ever I expected, but you've got all your profit tied up in horses and wagons. You might as leave try to sell firecrackers at Thanksgiving time as to try selling that kind of stuff now that harvest and thrashing is over. It wouldn't bring you half of what you paid for it."

With the rebuilding we'd done to the wagons, I knew they'd bring more than I'd put into them, but I told him, "That's right. That's why I'm not going to sell out, but keep everything over the winter."

"Now you're talking!" he said, and slapped me on the leg. "I've got things worked out so you can keep those ponies of yours busy right up to freezing time, and make yourself a scad of money."

It sounded to me like the deals he'd made for me on the broken-down old horses, wagons, and harness, but I said, "That's fine. I'm listening."

"Well, Son," he said, "the owner of that land Hudson had will let you have the whole kit and caboodle of it for next year; you to furnish the seed and take sixty percent of the crop, instead of a half, like Clara got. Of course, I'd lend you the money for seed, on notes running till next harvest time, and you'd make yourself a wealthy man." He unrolled the sheaf of papers, pushed it toward me, and asked, "Have you any notion what sixty percent of the wheat off those two sections brought?"

"Sure," I told him. "I brought the final statement from the elevator. It would amount to about thirty thousand dollars, after taking out thrashing and hauling. And as near as I can find out, it was the only crop worth harvesting that has been raised on that land in five years. I'm much obliged to you for the trouble you've gone to, but I'm going to let someone else gamble on that high divide wheat land." There was no reason for telling him that the owner had already offered me two-thirds of the crop if I furnished the seed, or that I'd leased the buildings and pasture.

Bones became a little huffy when I told him I didn't want the deal he'd been planning to cook up. He straightened in his chair, scowled at me, and asked gruffly, "What you aiming to do when you run out of hauling? Loaf?"

"No," I told him, "I don't care much about loafing. It looks as if Mrs. Hudson is going to have a pretty fair corn crop, and I've promised to harvest it for her. Until it's ready for shucking, I thought I might nose around a little and try my hand at the cattle business."

Bones got over his huffiness in two seconds. He leaned forward again, and told me, "That's the ticket, Son! We had a trader here, good cattleman too, but he's gone into the feeding business, so there's no trader this side of Oberlin, and there's

need for one. You work along close with me, and you could
make a scad of money. With me knowing all these farmers
hereabouts the way I do, I can tell you where to buy, and I'll
lend you whatever money you need, on eight percent paper
instead of ten. I'll do better than that for you, Son. I've got
a good section of pasture land right up here on the hills, best
place in the world for those horses of yours. I'll let you have it
for what it cost me, and you won't have to put a nickel down.
A man don't often sell a piece of land that way, but I like to
see an ambitious young man get off to a good start. We'll make
up the mortgage to cover what little other stuff you've got,
along with the land."

I kept my face straight, and tried to look as eager as I could
till he'd made his pitch, then told him, "You're certainly kind
to me—just like you were when you made those first deals for
me on horses and wagons—but I can't afford it. I'll play along
on my own."

Bones glared at me till I grinned, then he grinned too, and
said, "All right, Son, we talk the same language. You know the
fix I'm in with some of these cattle farmers. What I need is a
trader in this valley who will work close with me, buy some of
the cattle I've got mortgages on but don't want to foreclose,
ship 'em, and help me get my money out. You play along with
me and I'll give you all the help I can, and the only edge I'll
take on you will be the interest; that'll be eight per cent."

I'd never thought about going into the cattle trading business. It had been my plan to buy a couple of dozen good yearling
Hereford heifers, winter them along with the horses, and use
them as my start in building a herd. But the cattle trading
business sounded good to me, and I wasn't worried about the
possibility that Bones might try to take the long end of any
deals we made together. Any man is entitled to take the long
end of the stick when dickering if the other fellow is careless
enough to let him have it. What worried me was that Bones
might squeeze the farmers whose mortgages he held, tight

enough that they wouldn't be anxious to sell. After I'd thought about it a couple of minutes, I told him, "I'll give it a try on just one condition; that I can pay the farmers one-third of the price in cash."

"A quarter," he said quickly, like an auctioneer trying to run up a bid.

"No," I told him, "a third. Otherwise you find yourself another cattle trader."

Instead of answering, Bones stuck his hand out to shake.

When Judy and I had finished our bookkeeping that evening, I told her I planned to go into the cattle trading business, and of the deal I'd made with Bones. She became as excited as she was when the hauling business went over the top, danced around the kitchen, and wanted to know if it would be all right if she told her folks. "Sure," I told her. "The more people who know about it the better. If those who want to sell come looking for me, instead of my going to look for them, I'll have a trading advantage."

During the next couple of weeks it was easy for me to see that Judy had proved the old saying, "Telaphone, telagraph, or tell a woman." Whenever I didn't need the old Maxwell she was out on the roads with it, and she must have told every farmer within fifteen miles of Cedar Bluffs that I'd pay him a third in cash for any cattle mortgaged to Bones. I could seldom take a load of wheat to town without having some farmer stop me on the road, or wait for me at the elevator, and every one of them had cattle to sell.

I was greener than a frog about the cattle trading business, but there were a few things I did know; I'd have to buy my cattle by the head, and sell them by the pound, at auction, when they reached the big city stockyards. Then too, I would have to pay for freight, feeding on the way, and the commission agent's fee.

I had Judy get me a Kansas City paper at McCook, so I could check on the most recent prices being paid for various grades of cattle at the auctions. Then I talked to the depot agent at The Bluffs, and found out that freight and feeding would cost about a cent and a quarter a pound. Allowing another quarter-cent for commission, I could figure out how much a pound I could afford to pay, but that wasn't too much help when I had to buy by the head. I'd have to guess at the weights, and if I guessed too high on high-priced cattle I could lose my eye teeth. I decided that I'd start off by shipping skinny old cows for my first carload. They were the cheapest cattle on the list, selling for $3\frac{1}{2}¢$ a pound, so it wouldn't break me if I guessed wrong by as much as a thousand pounds on a carload.

I made one more check before I did any buying. From having my wagons weighed at the elevator, I knew the exact weight of each one, so we loaded the two skinniest cows I'd bought from Mrs. Hudson—one on each wagon of my rig— and I drove them down to the elevator for weighing. By studying them carefully after I brought them back, I got a pretty good idea of what almost any skinny old cow would weigh.

During the first eight days of October Judy and I kept the old Maxwell on the run every hour between my morning and evening hauling trips, and I must have dickered on more than a hundred skinny old cows. Most of the farmers wanted more than their cows were worth, but by the afternoon of the eighth I'd bought thirty at prices I thought I could afford to pay. I got only one from some farmers, but two or three from others, and told them all to deliver their cows to the shipping pen at Cedar Bluffs late Saturday afternoon. Then I stopped at the depot, and left an order for a cattle car to be set off at the chute when the noon train went west.

Friday fell on October 10th, and the axe fell on my hauling business. Late that afternoon Ted Harmon pulled his thrashing rig out of the last field, and I started Doc off for the elevator with little more than half a load. The first of the next week we'd have a dozen or so loads to haul from a small machine, but Paco and I could take care of that, and Paco was going to stay with me for the winter. He'd help me reshingle the barn to make a place for storing our wagons and harness, and keep an eye on the stock while I was busy with my cattle trading business. The rest of the crew decided they'd go to Denver next day, taking the afternoon express from McCook, so that Friday night I rented the pitcher's flivver again.

Saturday morning Paco hung the harnesses away, and turned the horses we would no longer need out to pasture, while the other fellows packed their gear, and Judy and I figured up the books and wrote checks. Gus, Lars, and Judy had drawn nothing, so her check was for $966; $256 for her share of the harvest money, and $10 for every day since the end of July. Theirs were $4.50 higher, because of splitting my first day's pay. Paco's check was for $956, and both Bill and Jaikus had well over $900 coming. Doc had drawn the most, but still had $876 due him. When I wrote his check I made it for $926, and when I handed it to him I told him the extra fifty was for the clothes I'd ruined. At first he didn't want to take it, and said I'd done him a favor by ruining them, but when I told him I'd still have a good cash profit left he was glad enough to have the extra money.

I did have a good cash profit, too; far beyond anything I'd thought I could possibly make. I'd paid off my second note to Bones, my grocery and team-hiring bills, spent $512 for my skinny old cows, sent $200 to my mother, and when I'd collected for the hauling job we'd just finished, would have $1,156 in the bank.

It was nearly noon before we got started for McCook; Judy driving Gus, Lars, and Old Bill in the Maxwell, and I followed with Doc, Jaikus, and Paco in the flivver. I'd called the hotel in McCook so they'd have a fine dinner ready for us, and we must have been at the table two hours—just remembering and talking about little things that happened during the summer. Then all but Paco and Judy excused themselves and went out, saying they wanted to cash their checks and buy their railroad tickets.

They were gone more than half an hour, then Doc came hurrying back into the dining room, fumbling in his pockets. "Did you notice if I left my watch on the kitchen table?" he asked Judy. "I can't find it any place, and I wanted to set it by the depot clock, so we won't risk missing the train."

Judy and I both knew there hadn't been any watch left on the table, because we'd cleared it off when we put the books away.

"Never mind," Doc said when we'd told him, "I'll pick up another one when I get to Denver. Let me borrow yours, Bud, so I can set the right time on it."

Doc hadn't had time to go farther than the lobby before the whole crew came trooping back into the dining room. I wasn't surprised to see that they were all carrying packages for Judy, but I had a hard time to keep from bawling like a baby when they all crowded around my chair, and Doc handed me back my watch. It was a seventeen-jewel Waltham.

I felt almost like a man who has lost his family when the train pulled out, and I'd probably have felt worse if we hadn't had to hurry right back to The Bluffs, to load out my first shipment as a cattle trader.

All thirty of the old cows were in the shipping pen when we got there, bawling and probably feeling about as I had when I watched the Denver express pull out of McCook. Only one old sister gave us any trouble in loading. She had no intention of leaving her native land, and to get her up the chute and into the car, Paco had to twist her tail while I hauled her along by the horns.

We'd barely closed and bolted the door when the eastbound freight whistled as it pulled away from Trear, so I had to run back to the depot and get my bill of lading made out. It took only a few minutes to uncouple the engine, pull my car from the siding, and couple it into the train. Then the engineer blew a couple of toots on the whistle, to call in the flagman, and my first shipment was on its way to Kansas City.

It was just a carload of skinny old cows, but I was as proud as if it had been prime steers. I think Judy was proud, too. We stood on the depot platform, with her arm tucked under mine, and watched until the train disappeared beyond the wooded curve of Beaver Creek. By my Waltham, it was exactly 6:13.